Gerhard Preyer
Intention and Practical Thought

Gerhard Preyer

Intention and Practical Thought

HUMANITIES
ONLINE

Bibliographic information published by the Deutsche Nationalbibliothek

The Deutsche Nationalbibliothek lists this publication in the
Deutsche Nationalbibliografie; detailed bibliographic data are available
in the Internet at http://dnb.d-nb.de

© 2011 Humanities Online
Frankfurt am Main, Germany
www.humanities-online.de
info@humanities-online.de

ISBN 978-3-941743-09-0

Cover: Uwe Adam, Bruchköbel
Printed in Germany

E-Book edition available on our website: www.humanities-online.de

Contents

To Wang Jan-ming (Wang Shou-jen)

Geographical Overview
Analytical Philosophy of Action

> *The difference here between a human being and an animal lies in the possibility of the human being expressing his intention and putting into words his intention to do so-and-so, for his own benefit or for the benefit of others.*
>
> S. Hampshire[1]

> *Action is the philosophical sibling of perception, and hence of epistemology. Both compel us to face the problem of the relation between the mind and the body, thought and the world.*
>
> D. Davidson[2]

The analytical theory of action has a long history now already. It had reached its peak in the 1970s years. But in after years there are re-systematizations and continuations.[3] Firstly I sketch as overview the main problems in this field and also those of practical reasoning because they are not remembered very well, and further on I will give some particular answers to the questions and solutions in this context. The leading questions of the theory of actions are:

What are actions? What are intentional actions? How are intentional actions to explain as intentional one? What is the relationship between intentions, intentional actions and intending? Is there something like a class of intentional actions?

E. Anscombe made a distinction between the *expression of intention* as a prediction, for example, "I am going to do that-and-that" (act-

---

1 S. Hamsphire, Thought and Action. New York 1959, 98.

2 Davidson, Aristotle's Action, 277. In: Truth, Language, and History. Oxford 2005.

3 For example, A.R. Mele, Springs of Action. Understanding Intentional Behavior. Oxford 1992, Self-Deception Unmasked. Princeton 2001, Effective Intention. The Power of Conscious Will. Oxford 2009, Effective Intentions. The Power of Conscious Will. Oxford 2009, R. Tuomela, The Philosophy of Social Practices. A Collective Acceptance View. Cambridge 2002, J. Nida-Rümelin, Strukturelle Rationalität. Ein philosophischer Essay über praktische Vernunft. Stuttgart 2001, G.H. von Wright, Normen, Werte und Handlungen. Frankfurt am Main 1994.

ing with an intention), *intentional action* (acting intentionally), and *with what intention things are done* (intending to act).[4] The problem is whether one of these distinctions involves the whole topic when analyzing intention in general. But it is obvious that this is not easy to show because if we argue that intentions always concern the future, intentional actions which are not being directed to the future are not explained. Therefore the connection of *intention* and *intentional* in ordinary talk is put in question. Anscombe argues that it is implausible to assume that the word *intention* is equivocal and occurs in different cases.[5] The following must be explained:

What is the relationship between *intention, intentional action*, and *intending*? What distinguishes *intention, intentional actions*, and *actions that are not done intentionally*?

Normally we say that an intentional action is done with an intention. The opposite of intentional is unintentional, that is, with no intention. But between these two there is a "not unintentional" doing, for example, Hamlet killed the man behind the arras intentionally but he does not have the intention to kill Polonius.[6] It goes back to Anscombe that there is no fundamental description of doings and events as intentional actions as such, but that we describe them as *intentional* under some descriptions.[7] She introduced a new question asking, "How are different actions related?". Anscombe's and Davidson's (and D.S. Shwayder) answer to the question is that the relation of various actions is *one of identity under descriptions*. We may call that the *Anscombe-Davidson view*. Davidson adds the problem of the ontology of action because we refer to the same (single) event. When we say that Peter's killing of Smith was cruel, then there is an event which makes the sentence true. Yet, this leads us on to the problem whether these descriptions are singular terms, and whether adverbial modifications are identical

4 *Expressions* be viewed as acoustical or two-dimensional geometric shapes of actual utterances or inscriptions and as abstract entities (classes of utterances or inscriptions without exemplification) Davidson, The Second Person (1992), 107-08. In: Subjective, Intersubjective, Objective. Oxford 2001.

5 E. Anscombe, Intention. Oxford 1957, 1-12. On intentions and action: Hampshire, Thought and Action, 90-168.

6 Davidson, Agency (1980): 46. In: Actions and Events. Oxford 1980, G.H. von Wright, Das Verstehen von Handlungen – Disputation mit Georg Meggle. In: Normen, Werte und Handlungen. Frankfurt am Main 1994, 171-72.

7 Anscombe, Intention, 29.

with adjectival modifications when we accept events as a part of our everyday life ontology. But the problem is that there is no simple way of distinguishing between intentional and non-intentional deeds. Both are not to distinguish by observation only. Many philosophers agree in that *intentional actions are to define as done by the agent*

1. *for* a reason: *A* is done *for* a reason only if reason *is* a cause of *A*, for example, A. I. Goldman, Davidson.[8]
2. But this is to distinguish from the intention (reason) *with which* an agent did what he did.

The answer to the question, "Why was *x* done?" mentions an intention as directed to a future state of affairs. The description of a future state of affairs is in itself an answer to this question and expresses an intention. The problem of cause versus reason emerges because the answer to the question does not refer to the past.[9] It is often argued that from this claim the principal question arises, "What are the conditions under which it is true that actions were done *for* a reason?"[10] *It is also accepted among philosophers that intentions are the link between reasons and actions.*

1. The question, "How do we describe action?" was answered by the so-called *two language* argument as a reply to the Humean answer. This problem was put in the context of a further question:
     What is the relation between the description of actions and the propositional content of explained attitudes, provided that these attitudes stand in a relation to such descriptions, and how can we explain actions with these attitudes? Are reasons for actions—like beliefs, motives, intentions, or wills—causes or not?
     This is the task of the so-called *explanation by redescription.*[11] In cognitive and also practical inferences the word *because* has two senses:

8 'A' is to read for an action variable for actions, in this book.
9 Anscombe, Intention, 34-41.
10 A.R. Mele, Springs of Action, 6-7.
11 Davidson, Problems in the Explanation of Action (1987), 105. In: Problems of Rationality. Oxford 2004. It is to emphasize that Davidson makes the distinction between explanatory and non-explanatory redescription by the purpose, that is, the intention. An intention is, for him, *not a part of actions*, but a cause, 105.

(a) In deductive inferences it signifies a logically necessary relationship between the premises and the accepted conclusion, and

(b) a causal relation exists between the beliefs of the thinker/speaker and his acceptance of the conclusion by the valid premises, and shortly after that he accepts the conclusion. This is not a causal relation of the *arguments* but the causal relations of the *events* they describe.[12]

The word *because* in sentences like "... did ... because ..." is interpreted as *logical* (not causal), *causal* or, in a particular way, *logical and causal*.

Hume-causes or *Hume-explanations* are supported by general regularities. G. Ryle, Anscombe, R.S. Peters, H.L.A. Hart and A.M. Honore, A.I. Melden, N. Malcolm, C. Taylor, G.H. v. Wright, P.F. Strawson, G. Wilson and others have argued that the explanations by reasons and a causal explanation are logically different accounts in nature.[13] Actions are not to explain by statements of law about the connection between belief and intention in general. There is a *logical (conceptual)* relationship between an agent's *intending* to do something A and his A-doing. The explanation of intentional behavior *requires a concept of intention*. Doing something like "going native", for example, is a case or instance of *intentional* behavior of going native only in case that an agent has going native *thoughts*, that is, a belief that some activities are going native, other do not, and so on. These are no causal relations but conceptual ones. Davidson, Danto, A.I. Goldman, A.C. MacIntyre, A.J. Ayer, S.E. Toulmin and others reject this, and they

12 A.I. Goldman, A Theory of Human Action. Englewood Cliff 1970, 100-01.

13 G. Ryle, Concept of Mind. New York 1949, Anscombe, Intention, R.S. Peters, The Concept of Motivation. London 1958, H.L.A. Hart, A.M. Honore, Causation in Law. London 1959, A.I. Melden, Free Action. London 1960, N. Malcolm, Consciousness and Causality. In: D.M. Armstrong, N. Malcolm eds, Consciousness and Causality. Oxford 1984, 3-101, C. Taylor, Explanation of Behavior. London 1964, G.H. v. Wright, Explanation and Understanding. New York 1971, P.F. Strawson, Freedom and Resentment. Proceedings of the British Academy 1962; G. Wilson, The Intentionality of Human Action. Stanford 1989; on a critique of the logical-connection argument F. Stoutland, The Logical Connection Argument. American Philosophical Quarterly 7 1970, B. Aune, Metaphysics. The Elements. Minneapolis (1985) 2002[5], 191-96, see also G. MacDonald, P. Pettit, Semantics and Social Science, London 1981, 91- 93.

bring the explanation with reasons closer to a modified causal explana-tion.[14] In the *Elster-Davidson-Mele-version* there are *mixed accounts* between both.[15] This goes back to Davidson, who has modified his causal analysis of explanation of action. There are *two* different ways in which belief-desire pairs are related to actions:

(a) The logical relation is between the content of beliefs and desires and that something is desirable (valuable) about the action, and
(b) a causal relation between the reasons and the occurrence of the action.

With the first relation, Davidson conforms to the logical connection-argument. But it is far from clear what the causal relation between reasons and actions is.[16] Wright's theory of action is a version of a more *mixed account*, a so-called *Verstehens-account*: explaining actions by reasons is an understanding of action. But for him, desires and needs have also a causal effect on our behavior.[17] R. Tuomela gives an *argumentative*

---

14 Davidson, Action, Reasons, and Causes (1963). In: Actions and Events. Oxford 1980, A. Danto, Analytical Philosophy of Action. Cambridge 1973, A. I. Goldman, A Theory of Human Action. Englewood Cliff 1970, A. C. MacIntyre, A Mistake about Causality in Social Science. In: P. Las-lett, W. G. Runciman (eds.), Philosophy, Politics and Sociology II. Oxford 1962, A. J. Ayer, Man as a Subject for Science, August Comte Memorial Lecture 6. London 1964, S. E. Toulmin, Human Understanding. Princton 1972.
15 J. Elster, The Nature and Scope of Rational Choice Explanation. In: E. Lepore, MacLaughlin (eds.), Action and Events. Perspectives on the Philosophy of D. Davidson. New York 1985. Mele, Springs of Action, on the Elster-Davidson version, Rajeev Bhargava, Individualism in Social Science. Forms and Limits of a Methodology. Oxford 1992, 134-141, Davidson, Paradoxes of Irrationality (1982), 173. In: Problems of Ratio-nality.
16 On the problem of mental causation E. Rogler, G. Preyer, Anomalous Monism and Mental Causality. On the Debate of Donald Davidson's Philosophy of the Mental. Open Access: https://ssl.humanities-online.de/en/openaccess.php. It is a shorter version of E. Rogler, G. Preyer, Anom-aler Monismus und mentale Kausalität: Ein Beitrag zur Debatte über D. Davidsons Philosophie des Mentalen. In: Materialismus, anomaler Monismus und mentale Kausalität. Zur gegenwärtigen Philosophie des Mentalen bei D. Davidson und D. Lewis. Frankfurt am Main 2001.
17 Wright, Normen, Werte und Handlungen.

13

reconstruction in his critique on Wright and takes in the principles of the rational theory of decision in the explanation of action. The problem is which roles have general statement in the scheme of explanation of action.[18] *Understanding* is an ambiguous expression, for example, (a) as knowing how to do something, (b) of phenomena as an understanding of something (Kant: intelligere, that is, to know something by concepts), and (c) hermeneutical understanding, for example, of texts, gestures, and utterances as an understanding of something that was already understood. I use the expression *understanding* as understanding of something in continuation. Understanding of something as that-and-that is a belief that something is that-and-that which can be false.

A specific question of a semantic analysis of the description of actions was introduced with the so-called *accordion-effect* (J. L. Austin, J. Feinberg).[19] It means that an action can "be squeezed down to a minimum" or "else stretched out" like the musical instrument. "Because of the *accordion-effect* we can usually replace any ascription to a person of causal responsibility by an ascription of agency or authorship"[20], but this property is *only* a feature of description of actions and not of actions themselves[21]. The *accordion-effect* gives us no answer to the question whether the action we ascribe was done intentionally.[22]

The description of action further leads us to the question:

How does an interpreter identify intentions? Are actions and intentions items that differ really or logically? How can we explain that the same movement of my hand has different actions and occasions as consequences?

The latter question leads us to the distinctions of *act-constitutive principles* (Goldman: act-generation). The fundamental problem in the theory of action is where an answer about the role of *intentions* can be found. For the traditional desire-belief versions, intentions are no original mental items.[23] I will argue in the following that this account is to modify.

18 R. Tuomela, Human Action and Its Explanation. Dordrecht 1977. Davidson, Hempel on Explaining Action (1976), 261-75. In: Actions and Events has given a particular answer of the problem.

19 J. L. Austin, A Plea for Excuses. Proceedings of Aristotelian Society Vol. 57 1959, J. Feinberg, Action and Responsibility (1965). In: A. L. White (ed.), Philosophy of Action. London 1968.

20 Feinberg, Action and Responsibility (1965), 106.

21 Aune, Reason and Action. Dortrecht 1977, 5.

22 On the *accordion-effect*, I 1. (a), in this book.

23 For example, Davidson, R. Audi, Bearsley, W. Davis give *desire-belief*

2. Hart has argued in his classic article *The Ascription of Responsibility and Rights* (1949) that we do not use the description of actions descriptively but ascriptively.[24] The basic notion is his *concept of defeasibility*. This account is well known under the name *ascriptivism*.[25] It is the aim of Davidson's analysis of sentences on propositional attitudes to show that, on the contrary, the *individuation of actions* is a matter of an attributive ascription, such is, the agent has certain features we ascribe. This is caused by the ontological and analytical question of analysis of description of action in different vernaculars with the example of reference of singular terms. For *Davidson's version* of a total theory the ascription of actions, linguistic or not, is to justify together with the individuation of propositional attitudes by distal stimuli in the triangulation. In this respect the ascription of actions lead us back to radical interpretation and its event-ontology because the questions,

What are actions? Are actions mental causes, physical effects, or a connection between both? How do actions differ from other events? How do we individuate actions?

are motivated by an introduction of an *ontological commitment* in the theory of language: the world consists of events as particulars, they cannot be reduced.

There are three more questions we must ask:

Are actions body movements? Are they identical with the normal physiological process? And which role do intentional body movements play for the analysis of action?

The answer to these questions is of particular significance because by them we assign ontological decisions in the theory of language and action. This is the case exactly when we are concerned with analyzing the reference to descriptions of action along with the *individuation of acts*. The different accounts of act-individuation are connected with the *problem of event individuation*. The *coarse-grained individuation* (Anscombe, Davidson) and the *fine-grained individuation* (Goldman and others) have also consequences for the mental concepts and for ontology because for mental concepts the individuation of events is relevant.

analyses of intention. On Davidsons modification Problems in the Explanation of Action (1987). In: Problems of Rationality.

24 H.L.A. Hart, The Ascription of Responsibility and Rights. In: Proceedings of Aristotelian Society, XLIX 1949.

25 On critique from a Fregean and Humean point of view, P. Geach, Ascriptivism. In: Logic Matter. Oxford 1992.

The hard core of Davidson's analysis of the logical form of action sentences is the identity-thesis and the coarse-grained individuation of events because of the claim to show how we immediately instantiate an action to an agent.[26] The *semantic opacity* of the attribution of intention gives us a hint how we understand intentional actions. "Hamlet intentionally kills the man behind the arras, but he does not intentionally kill Polonius. Yet Polonius is the man behind the arras, and so Hamlet's killing of the man behind the arras is identical with his killing of Polonius. It is a mistake to suppose there is a class of intentional action: if wee took this tack, we should be compelled to say that one and the same action was both intentional and not intentional."[27] *The criterion of agency is semantically intensional and the expression of agency is extensional: there is an agent who brings about something we can be described under the feature that makes it intentionally.* Therefore we can speak of *classes of events* that are actions.[28] This is the *syncategorematical account of intention.* Actions are intentional body movements, and the relation between agent and the event that is performed is not dependent on the descriptions of the items. His concept of primitive action is a critique of Danto's distinction between basic and non-basic actions and his causal interpretation of the act-pair *A-A'*.

3. *Events* play an important role in our ontology. They are significant for the analysis of mental and physical acts, linguistic acts, probability theory, and also systems of metaphysics.[29] For the theory of action, versions of *act*-individuation are connected with the question of *event-individuation* in general and with sorts of vocabulary we use for that. The theory of events is at the same time involved in the explanation of the mental to the physical. There are three views from which the *problem of act-individuation* can be answered:

26 Preyer, Donald Davidson's Philosophy. From Radical Interpretation to Radical Contextualism, Frankfurt am Main 2011[2], on the logical form of action sentences, singular causal relations and the ontological commitment of events, 168-192.
27 Davidson, Agency (1971), 46, 46-47. In: Action and Events. Oxford 1980.
28 Davidson, Agency (1971), 46-47. In: Action and Events.
29 On a theory of events, R.M. Martin, Events, Reference and Logical Form. Washington D.C. 1978.

(a) the *coarse-grained* view (Quine, Davidson),
(b) the *fine-grained* view (Goldman, J. Kim), and
(c) the *componential* view (I. Thalberg).[30]

For the *coarse-grained* view mental events are token-identical with the physical event essentially, that is, the same event is described and picked out under physical and mental descriptions. Therefore the firing of particular neurons, for example, forms a particular intention. The *fine-grained* view rejects this monism because mental properties are not identical with physical ones: therefore, *different properties mean different events.* This leads to the *problem of mental causality.* I think it cannot be solved in contemporary philosophy and researches. But many philosophers agree with that, and this is difficult to reject that the use of the expression *Agent has a reason to A* ascribes a mental state to an agent. This leads us to the question, "What sort of theory of action is possible?" [31]

Peter flips the switch, turns on the light, and illuminates the room. The paradigmatic leading question of the individuation of action is:

How many acts have been carried out?

The identity-thesis is that there is only *one* action, but in our example three descriptions are given.[32] This follows from the coarse-grained individuation of actions. An event is an action if it is caused by agent causation unmediatedly and is, as an action, independent of its description. The analysis of logical form of action sentences and the interpretation of singular causal statements claim to commit us to the ontology of coarse-grained events, and it is at the same time connected with the rejection of the logical connection-argument. This is the *syncategorematic account of intentions* at the beginning of the inner-theoretical history of the *unified theory* of thought, meaning, action and evaluation (= Unified Theory).[33] *Davidson's conception of primary reasons, a belief and a pro*

30 Preyer, Donald Davidson's Philosophy, on the logical connection argument 200-04, on Davidson's primary reasons, 212-39, on Danto's basic acts, 205-11, on Thalberg, 252-57, on Goldman, 257-67, on Davidson and Hempel, 274-77, on body movements and actions as events and their causation, 267-74.

31 In this proposal I go along with Aune, Reason and Action. Dordrecht 1977.

32 Davidson, D. S. Shwayder and others. The thesis goes back to Anscombe, Intention, 45-6.

33 Davidson, Action, Reasons, and Causes (1963). In: Action and Events. Oxford 1980, 3-19.

attitude, claims to give us an answer to the question, what does a causal explanation of action mean? For his theory of belief and meaning the concept of reason plays a particular role: pro attitudes and beliefs are the causes of action; they have causal power. Such reason is a complex disposition (states in persons) which causes a free and intentional action as an event. The logical relation is only a matter of redescription of behavior in the light of the rationality of attitudes, and this is not relative to individual agents.

Goldman, in difference to the coarse-grained view, has a *fine-grained view*. The alternative to a coarse-grained individuation of action tokens is that in our example "Peter" has performed three acts with distinct act properties. Another view is Thalberg's *componential* view arguing that the action of "Peter" has various components like, for example, moving his arm, flipping the switch, and so on.

The question is whether there is something like a theory of action and whether descriptions of action (action sentences) are to analyze as singular terms in principle. The problem is that the standard views of desire, beliefs, intention and the like are too fine-grained or too coarse-grained.[34] But it is not disputed that it is to make the distinction between intentional and non-intentional behavior and just this is not possible without an intentionalistic vocabulary.

It has been a result of these debates that now we have to distinguish between the explanation of action and of other *human events* like, for example, "to flush", "to fluster", "to be confused", *states* like, for example, "to be stupid", *expectations* like, for example, "to hold a promise", *feelings* like, for example, "fear", "pleasure", *faults*, and *omissions*.

4. The proposals of interpretation of *practical reasoning* are developed outside the moral science. The proposals were inspired by the research in the mathematical and psychological theory of decision. Beginning with Ascombe's *Intention* (1957) the analysis of practical inferences had been of a new significance, and there is an extensive debate about the validity of such inferences.[35] *Firstly*, it is to emphasize that the nature of such inferences is determined by the conclusion, that is, it is an action or an attempt. *Secondly*, the conclusion as an action goes along

34 Mele, Springs of Action, 40.
35 Anscombe, Intention, 57-72, G.H. von Wright, On so-called Practical Inference (1959). In: Raz (ed.), Practical Reasoning. Oxford 1978: 46-62. On Wright and Tuomela W. Stegmüller, Probleme und Resultate der Wissenschaftstheorie und Analytischen Philosophie, Bd. 1. Erklärung, Begründung, Kausalität. Berlin 1983, 487-92.

with an intention or is an expression of it. *Thirdly*, there is a deontic statement that something is to do or ought to be done. If the premises of the inference are true then they state a reason for doing something the agent is committed to. I think that the latter is not the case, and it is an error to think this way. *Fourthly*, rules of practical inferences do not correspond to rules of deduction. But this is also the case with inductive inferences. The problem is whether we need a particular logic for the evaluation of practical inferences. *Fifthly*, in the case of beliefs like "*x* beliefs *p*" the content of belief *p* does not disappear if we delete "*x* beliefs". If, in cases like "I want, intent, desire ... *p*", we delete the words "I", "want", "intend", then we have an incomplete speech. This is the problem of the *content of conative attitudes*.

Anscombe and also Davidson argue that the desire of an agent is not itself a premises in practical inferences. Therefore such inferences do not lead inevitably to an action, but they only indicate a desire, a belief or that something is intended.[36] Therefore the problem is whether practical inferences say something of the strength of reasons for doing something that an agent may have. I think that Davidson's analysis of practical inferences is right. The inference may describe the intention of an agent, but it does not inform us about his factual reasoning and says nothing about the desirability of an action. Davidson's *motivational strength thesis* "If an agent wants more to do *x* than he wants to do *y* and he believes himself free to do either *x* or *y*, then he will intentionally do *x* if he does either *x* or y intentionally" is no logical evaluation of practical inferences.[37] He further states a *judgment/motivation alignment thesis* that in most cases the agent is also motivated to follow his judgment what to do best. But the principle of *elimination of inconsistency* (practical inconsistency) and of *execution* as a non-logical principle is to introduce, we do not evaluate the practical inference, but the agent. The idea goes back to Anscombe: An agent can make faults in his doings and thoughts.[38]

36 On a summery on reasons and reasoning Raz, Introduction, 4-8. In: Raz (ed.), Practical Reasoning. Oxford 1978. I agree with Aune that we do not need a deontic logic and that practical inferences are to reduce to the formal logic of ordinary assertoric inference.

37 Davidson, How is Weakness of the Will Possible (1970), 23. In: Davidson 1980.

38 Anscombe, Intention, 56-7. The principle is also accepted by Aune. I introduced the *principle of execution* in one of my lectures at the end of seventies as a principle of the consistence of agent's execution as fulfilled, or not fulfilled.

In sum: we avoid confusions in so far as we distinguish evaluations of the agent as non-logical principles from the *concept of explanation*. The latter has an *own* subject of research.[39]

5. Davidson's Unified Theory is a *new foundation account of language* (this is his claim).[40] The theoretical framework relates the concepts of belief, desire, and linguistic meaning. *Belief* is treated in a *quantified form*, often calls *subjective probability*, and *desires* is measured in an *interval scale* like Fahrenheit temperature. It includes a version of what is called *decision theory*.[41] The Unified Theory's version of decision theory does not accept utilitarian consequentialism.[42] *The theory of decision is to connect by the theory of interpretation and communication because actions are to describe and explain as events, provided that they are consequences of a decision-theoretical structured set of attitudes.* The claim is that the theory is suitable to explain intentions and intentional actions that are behavior, no matter whether linguistic or not.

The Unified Theory describes an *abstract structure*. The effective structure between the theory of interpretation and decision is that the ascription of attitudes is comparable to the measurement of different extent. Following R. Carnap, pairing numbers to entities enables us to

39 This is emphasized by Stegmüller, Probleme und Resultate der Wissenschaftstheorie und Analytischen Philosophie, Bd. 1., 487.
40 Preyer, Donald Davidson's Philosophy, on the Unified theory, 249-52, see also E. Lepore, K. Ludwig, Donald Davidson. Meaning, Truth, and Reality. Oxford 2005, 248-62, on the revised procedure of radical interpretation, 257-60.
41 We distinguish in ordinary science between *nominal* scales, like pairing numerical distinctions between individuals (attributes), for example, numbered colors by coffee cups, *ordinal* scales, like pairing an ordering relation on individuals (attributes), for example, grades of hardness, *interval* scales, like assigning numbers thereby differences between numbers reflect differences of the attributes being measured, *ratio* scales, like keeping of both: differences and ratios of quantities, that is, adding to an interval scale an absolute origin, for example, measurement of length in any unit (feet, meters), and *absolute* scales, like assigns numbers to entities, that is, all properties of the number reflect comparable (analogous) properties of the attribute, for example, in stating numbers to count votes for candidates, see Lepore, Ludwig, Donald Davidson, 243-45.
42 Davidson, The Objectivity of Values (1995), 41. In: Problems of Rationality.

making statements about sizes, weights, lengths etc. When doing this we do not identify entities like, for example, "The speed at which my car can drive" and "100 miles per hour". The ascription of attitudes and measured values is analogous because we do not multiply the entities. It is sufficient that they have a structure within which we can represent their properties of speeds, weights or attitudes, whatever. Numbers are a suitable means of expression and representation. The entities which have such a structure in the case of the ascription of attitudes are *sentences*. Davidson's proposal is that an oral or written utterance is the entity (content) with which an interpreter ascribes attitudes. That is his paratactic explanation of the ascription of attitudes. Therefore we use Ockham's razor for the ascription of attitudes, and we will not multiply our ontology for the ascription of attitudes without reasons. Sentences are the only measure of the ascription of attitudes and the mental.

The *abstract structure* of the theory includes a *representational theorem* and a *uniqueness theorem*. With the first we assign numbers to *beliefs and desires*, with the second we assign *numbers* to *measure probabilities* that constitute a ratio scale and to *desires* that constitute an *interval scale*. The distinction between both the scales goes back to F. M. Ramsey. The part of the theory which copes with linguistic meaning ascribes truth-conditions to all sentences of the speaker under study. The *unification* of the two theories depends on the fact that *the decision theory extracts cardinal utilities* and *subjective probabilities from simple preferences*, and *subjective probabilities applied to sentences* are sufficient to develop a theory of meaning.[43] In many cases we use *preference* with the meaning of "*x* is better like *y*". The Unified Theory makes the assumption that meaning, beliefs, and desires conspire. If we make the assumption that by a speaker (agent) choices we recognize the preferences that a significant set of his uttered sentences are true, then it follows from that resulting total theory of interpretation of uttered sentences that we ascribe beliefs and desires to the speaker. The Unified Theory applies *Jeffrey's version of decision theory* to sentences "a rational agent cannot prefer both a sentence and its negation to a tautology, nor a tautology to both a sentence and its negation".[44]

Building the theory of interpretation is not a building-block theory but a holistic one. Therefore we weigh the set of attitudes by the principle of charity. The theory assigns the *content* to beliefs, utterances, and

43 On the concept of preference, see II 1., 2. (a), in this book.
44 Davidson, Could There Be a Science of Rationality? (1995), 127. In: Problems of Rationality. Oxford 2004.

value simultaneously because the basic attitudes are interdependent. This holism is the characteristic of a *scheme of measurement*. *Desires* that we express by *preferences* are *conceptually basic attitudes*. The conceptual priority is reasoned thereby because we can conclude from a detailed knowing of the desires to the beliefs but not to the contrary. However, it is a strong requirement that belief and desire are to describe by their semantic contents. These contents imply that the *desirability of the action* is judged from the agent's point of view. The hard core of Davidson' Unified Theory is *Bayesian*. The *basics of evaluation* are desire (basic interests) and belief. The *subjective evaluation function* (utility function) is interpreted over *states* (propositions, events) *as desirable*, and the *probability function* represents the *disposition (expectation) of an individual agent* that a future event *will be happen*. Intentions as rational ones are connected with decisions, and they are nothing but desire-belief pairs. The *coherence of desirability* is not absolute but a rational policy of the evaluation of alternatives that the individual actor has. The problem in general is whether *optimized utility functions* (evaluation) are *desirability functions* in every case, that is, they describe the wants of an agent as reasons for actions.[45] In the history of his work Davidson has emphasized that all actions are intentional, no matter whether linguistic or not, and have unintended features and unexpected consequences. But the concept of intention does not modify acts directly. He has not given up the basic concept of "actions under a description" and the identity thesis.[46]

I think that the problem of Davidson's genial proposal is in principle whether it is the case that holism, externalism, and the normative feature of the mental stand or fall together in reality — in particular whether the common cause gives the content of attitudes globally. This leads back to the question he noted to the Bayesian theory of decision:

How can preferences and attitudes be described without identifying their content?

---

45 On critique J. Nida-Rümelin, Kritik des Konsequentialismus. München 1995, 36-45. R. Tuomela, Cooperation. Dordrecht 2000. On an interpretation of maximum expected desirability: B. Aune, Reason and Action, Dordrecht 1977, 137-42, on probability and supervenience Preyer, F. Siebelt, Reality and Humean Supervenience: Some Reflections on David Lewis' Philosophy, 12-16. In: Reality and Humean Supervenience Edited and Introduced by G. Preyer and F. Siebelt. Lanham 2001.

46 Davidson, Aristotle's Action (2001), 286-87. In: Truth, Language, and History. Oxford 2005.

This is the right question, but I think the epistemic restrictions limit the externalistic individuation of the content of attitudes by distal stimuli. This lead us back to the problem:

How do we assign content to words and attitudes to an agent externalistically?

Therefore, in the re-systematization and continuation of the Unified Theory the overall problem emerges whether the *a priori assumption of the principle of charity as a constraint of every interpretation* cannot guarantee the selection of the correct (univocal) correlation between behavior and its causation.

The truth-centered theory of meaning emphasized that linguistic meaning is not to analyze by a non-linguistic purpose or by the use of language. Whatever our option in the theory of meaning may be, this is not easy to revoke.

An answer must be given to the question:

What is the relation between beliefs, intentions, desires and intentional actions?

The main line of interpretation behavior is:

What was the reasoning, what were the presuppositions for the goal attainment of an agent with his conceptual resources?

I call this assumption the *presupposition of intelligibility of attitude*, and in so far as someone's utterances and actions are performed by such attitudes, they are comprehensible and can be re-interpreted within the same ontological framework that speaker (agent) and interpreter share. This does not exclude incontinent actions. We make this assumption for the ascription of actions.

How can explain a theory of interpretation linguistic behavior as actions, that is, *as* intentional?

The theory of interpretation and action has to interlock. If we want to explain what a speaker has done with his words, we have to know what the intended meaning of his uttered sentences was.

How far have we an evidence for the verification of our theory of interpretation of speech and action with the concept of intelligibility of attitudes?

A total theory of behavior cannot avoid presupposing the evaluation, measurement and fulfillment of attitudes from an agent's side. The ascription of attitudes works if the evidence for successful actions and communications is a convergence in ontology. The *explanatory redescription* makes the assumption: if we know the attitudes of an agent, his deliberation, and his ontological decision, then we understand this agent in a particular way from our description of his doings, that is, we describe his actions and doings as such that the agent has assumed that he satisfies his attitudes by his doings. If someone intends to perform an action, then an interpreter assumes that the agent has also certain beliefs *how* he can reach his goal.

What does an interpreter presuppose for the intelligible redescription of behavior and explanation by redescription?

An interpreter who draws out the assumption (implications) about the attitudes of the speaker (agent) for grasping the meaning of an utterance brings into play assumptions about the attitudes of him. In the case of an interpretation of an utterance, for example as an assertion, he supposes that the speaker intends to state something. But the assumption that the speaker has the attitude, the want, desire or goal orientation that explains his speech is more important. Normally the interpreter supposes that the speaker believes what he said, and wishes that the addressee recognizes his belief.

It is also accepted among many philosophers—comparable with the theory of interpretation—that a general answer of the ascription of action but not a solution case-by-case is required. The question is whether it works that an item of behavior counts as action if there is a description under which it is intentional and also if it is unintentional under other descriptions. *An explanation of intentional behavior as intentional must be given.* Therefore the intelligible redescription makes the assumption that we understand others like ourselves; and this is the only guarantee to redescribe intentional behavior *as* intentional.

In the next step—*Part I Enigmas of Agency I. The Reference of Action Description*—my subject is the analysis of descriptions and ascriptions of action. It is to show that we have to make a distinction between the application of the accordion effect, the theoretical conclusion from the description of behavior to a description of actions, and the ascription of *agent causality*. The ascription of attitudes is relevant because we bring into play such conceptual resources for the semantic interpretation of a speaker's utterances and parts of a given population, such is, the interpreter begins with the application of the principle that his interpretation refers to the same state of affairs, things and events to which the speaker is also referring—including the resultant action that follows from these circumstances.

If we begin to describe items of behavior in continuation as an action, our descriptions are *essentially incomplete*, and it is always an uncertainty to fix the positive values of such descriptions, such is, the ends and doings are not determined under certain conditions. We are confronted with the incompleteness of such descriptions. The best *prin-*

ciple to limit these descriptions is the *propositional expression*, that is, it is the case that ... In this sense we can apply the *accordion effect* to the descriptions of actions: each sequence that is squeezed down to a minimum or stretched out gives us a deed.

Intentions are the primary link between reasons and actions. Davidson's *syncategorematic account* is relevant because we can learn something from it in respect of its success but also of its failure.[47] Davidson has changed his *first version of primary reasons* and takes the explanation, the concept, and also the state of intention into play. Therefore the *second version of primary reasons* intentions and not only causal but also logical implication between the belief-desire pair as reasons and actions now taken as a serious subject of the theory of action.[48] But from my point of view he has not modified his account substantially because intentional actions are caused by our strongest beliefs that we express in all-out judgments. I call this the *problem of intention*.

The *syncategorematic account* has introduced the *identity-thesis* of action. Actions are events caused by an agent (agency as body movement) which is to describe as intentional. The ascriptions of attitudes are to *attribute* to the agent. I give an analysis what the difference between attributing and ascribing actions is. Take in the identity-theses and modify it at the same time. This leads me to A. I. Goldman's *critique of the identity thesis* of act, and the question, "What role play body movements as component of actions?" The theory of action as a theory is ontologically committed to events. *Explanatory redescription goes along with the question, "What sort of theory of action is possible?".* The answer to this question is a re-interpretation of explanatory redescription as a *theory of agent*, agency and its ascription, but not a re-interpretation of an ontology of events. Agents are instances; they are a component of our social ontology that we do not dispute in our object language about the social universe. They are not only individual but also social instances. This is analyzed in the debate about collective intentionality and belief and their ontology.[49]

47 Davidson, Action, Reasons, and Causes (1963), 3-19. In: Actions and Events. Oxford 1980.
48 Davidson, Problem s in the Explanation of Action (1987), 105-107. In: Problems of Rationality.
49 On the debate on collective beliefs and social ontology, see also ProtoSociology Vol. 18-19 2003: Understanding the Social II: Philosophy of Sociality. Edited by R. Tuomela, G. Preyer, G. Peter, Vol. 16 2002: Understanding the Social I: New Perspectives from Epistemology. On the use of

With taking the next step—2. *Explaining Actions*—I will show how the explanation of action is to analyze which takes in intentions as a link between reason and action. The proposals of interpretation of the explanation of action, practical thoughts and reasoning are developed outside moral science. The leading question was the problem of what sort the explaining action is, for example causal, teleological or intentional explanations. The proposals were inspired by research in the mathematical and psychological theory of decision. The leading questions were the *problem of reference of descriptions of action* and *the individuation of acts*, whether *reasons are causes*, and also the *validation of practical inferences*. First I give a re-interpretation of theoretical and practical thinking.

It is to explain *what beliefs and intentions are, whether they are states or not, and how the connection with both of them leads to the consequence of an action*. Practical thoughts imply intentions, but we have to distinguish between *thoughts* and *beliefs*. An answer to the *problem of intention* must be given. The explanation of action as an explanatory redescription by desires and beliefs includes different intentions. However, one must also find an answer to the question how the explanation of action fits in with the general approach of scientific explanations.

We describe actions if we give an answer to the question, "What was done?", and we ascribe actions if we ask for the authorship of the doing. If the ascription of actions takes off from its redescription, an interpreter assumes for it the ascription: x believes that a for z in y is required to reach his goal or bring about certain effects. To form an intention is also a matter of our beliefs, but intentions are self-referential. The ascription of something to an instance (speaker, agent), for example, going for a walk as done intentionally, assumes that the agent, for example, has "going for a walk" thoughts. If such an ascription is successful, it is assumed that the agent and the interpreter know fulfillment conditions and particular events as exemplifications of intentional behavior.

group-predicates and the debate on rejectionists: Preyer, What is wrong with Rejectionists, The Extension of G-Predicates, 237-63. In: Interpretation, Sprache und das Soziale. Philosophische Artikel. Frankfurt am Main 2005, see also Tuomela, The Philosophy of Sociality. The Shared Point of View, Oxford 2007, on "The Ontological Nature of Social Group" with reference to K. Mathiesen, 145-48, Tuomela, On Individualism and Collectivism in Social Science, S. R. Chant, A Dilemma for Non-Reductionist Accounts of Group Belief, both forthcoming.

We interpret *shall* as an expression of an attitude. From an agent's point of view, he has to distinguish between what he *intends* and *what* he achieves or doesn't. A person (agent) has knowledge without observation, and also the attempt must be separated from the report of his doing, that is, a particular knowledge about his *own* action. *Trying and intending play together.* This takes effect in the theory of interpretation from the third person point of view. We are confronted with the problem that an ascription of intentions like all other attitudes presupposes the application of the *principle of epistemic justice.* This is valid also in cases where our intentions go wrong and when they seem to be reasonable in social intercourse.

One must find an answer to the question what intentions and beliefs are and how the combination of both brings about an action. It is to show that practical thought implies intention. This explains us why the connection between belief and intention leads us to the structure of actions. If the inside of action, the self-reference and the attitudes, cannot be reached from outside (inside-outside differentiation), one cannot argue that there are no fulfillment conditions of doings we share. If we say that actions are doings, leave something alone, or refrain from doing something, they have *fulfillment conditions* as a *frame of reference.* The differentiation between *internal* and *external* is the generalized framework and is also the basic distinction that an observer (interpreter) makes for all explanatory redescription, that is, making behavior intelligible. Many philosophers have argued that it is absurd that there are propositions in our mind which we grasp internally. This may be right, but the inside-outside differentiation makes clear that the ascription of mental state and intending is not eliminable for making behavior intelligible. Doing goes together with intentions and an intended change, whatever may happen in the future.

I will show how the explanation of action is to analyze. At first one must find an answer of the question *what intentions and beliefs are* and *how the combination of both produces an action.* It is to show that *practical thoughts imply intentions.* To grasp this connection between belief and intention leads us to an explanation of actions and to an analysis of the word *because* in action explained sentence like "he/she/Peter/the group/the man in the other room ... did it *because* ...". The answer to the question, "What commitment gives the unconditional judgment its motivational strength?" connects the analysis of practical thought with practical reasoning.

In the next step—*Part II Practical Reasoning*—I will give an analysis of practical reasoning and an answer to the logical validity of practical inferences. The answer to the question, "Why did James x?" has clarified that, for example, "James" has the *conceptual resources* to act in correspondence with his practical reasoning (premises). It is to show that the analysis of practical thought and an intentional explanation of action give us an interpretation of the scheme of action that is represented in a practical inference. Yet, an answer concerning the *validity* of such reasoning must also be given.

How is the relationship between choosing, deciding, intending to determinate? What is the principle for evaluating the performance of actions?

In this context we come upon applying the *principle of execution of intentions and of fulfillment conditions of attitudes* (compliance — obedience and response conditions — and truth conditions) making behavior intelligible. The principle expresses the *decidedness* of an agent when he has said "I shall do x surely (really)". This is not a theoretical certainty of a prediction.

However, what is the relationship between *beliefs* and the *motivation* of actions?

The answer to these questions leads us back to Hume and Aristotle. All this shows us how the problem cannot be eliminated theoretically: it is not ex ante to exclude that a desire and a belief may cause an action in some cases but in other cases the result of our deliberation is a prima facie judgment. We are confronted with that: beliefs about the conditions of satisfaction on the application of practical inferences cannot be explained by *prima facie judgments* of "satisfied", "good", "correct". The problem is whether a stronger judgment is required for the evaluation of practical inferences, as Davidson has argued. I will argue, with a practical conclusion: we can state an intention, but we do not grasp the factual reasoning of the thinker by practical inferences, and we are not committed to do something by the logical force of practical reasoning.

In this context *incontinence* (weakness of the will) is to re-interpret. I agree with many philosophers that they are genuine *moral dilemmas* which are not to trivialize. For example, it is not to exclude that from true premises of practical inferences follows a contradiction because, for example, I hold my promise given to Pia to be punctual but I break my word given to Maria that I will never meet my old girlfriend, whatever the consequences may be. In so far the scheme of practical inferences describes in what respect an action can be, but need not be, the result of a reasonable deliberation. But the scheme is not a procedure to evaluate actions, nor a method to decide what I ought to do.

In so far as explanations by reasons entail laws, they are nothing but generalizations that we imply for an ascription of dispositions. But, in difference to C. Hempel, these laws are only valid for individuals which means that they are generalizations for the ascription of attitudes and traits of character that make such ascriptions informative for us. This is Davidson's answer to Hempel. The problem is that the *generalizations* that connect reasons and action are *not* laws that have the power of predictions. It is not to exclude that an agent does not only have an alternative reasoning and option and can decide in different ways, but it may also be that our ex-post considerations show that the reason which we ascribe to an agent was one reason among many others. Such generalizations are always hypothetical. But these explanations imply empirical generalizations.

In particular the exploring of the relation among the mental concepts as the psychological environment leads us to a *unified theory of social systems* and the ascription of attitudes and actions.[50] Furthermore, the analysis of intentions, motives, will—if there is something like a "will"—and the moral knowledge (commitments) is essential to understand agency and the social. This explains us also the role of language. Language is cognitively neutral. Neurological, physiological factors are outside the social and communication. We do not reach the consciousness of others. Every theory of social systems and of communication has to show that they can work without that. Behavior may be caused by external factors basically, and intentions are directed and point out something by external circumstances; but to explain behavior intentionally lingual ascription and attribution is necessary from the observer's side in a way in which they are not a conceptual distinction between both the observer and the agent. If there is a conceptual distinction between both, relativism is not disputed, and we cannot explain communication.

Teaching about what actions happen in a *social frame of reference* is observed and described by the participants by means of the borderlines of this framework and therefore from the social system point of view. The social frame is not global in respect to particular communications, but the frame of references of social systems is. The distinction between the frame of reference (the social system) and its environment is drawn by the members continuously. If it isn't, such systems and also communication would disappear. It is Davidson's claim to give us a *total theory*

---

50 On the framework Preyer, Soziologische Theorie der Gegenwartsgesellschaft (3 vol.) III Mitgliedschaft und Evolution, Wiesbaden 2008, 38-60.

of behavior, linguistic or not, by the fusion of the theory of interpretation and the theory of decision. The *homogeneity of interpretation* of
behavior, linguistic or not, is not an analysis of rational attitudes by the
application of the a priori constraint of the charity but the principle
fixes the conceptual resources by compositionality and the ontology
we suppose. *From my point of view the circle of belief and meaning is
not to compensate for the stimulus meaning, nor for the distal (common) cause.* The theory of interpretation and action has to interlock in
such a way that, if we want to explain what a speaker has done with
his words, we have to know: what is the intended meaning (content) of
his uttered sentences? But all interpretation supposes an *interest* about
making behavior intelligible.

Davidson extends the Unified Theory also to the analysis of *values*
(evaluations). From the point of view of radical interpretation he gives
an answer to the question why values are objectively but not ontologically real. From his point of view they are something we *have.* I will give
a particular answer to this problem. Speakers express value-commitments in utterances about what is desirable, correct, right, and so on.
We express such commitments in prescriptions like desirable, correct,
ought to, or with the use of evaluative expressions like good, cruel, boring, generous, and so on. These expressions are used in circumstances
where we utter advice and recommendations. We refer to value-commitments also to ascribe reasons of actions, for example, he has no reason
to do it because he was not committed. I argue against the account that
there is an equivalence between descriptive and normative expressions,
and normative acts do not describe anything. Value-predicates are no
names of properties, but speakers refer to criteria of application with
their utterances of such words. The interpretation of such utterances
supposes that the value-judgment is open to corrections. This leads me
also to the limits of justification. The role of values and commitment is
to analyze in a new way from the social systems point of view.[51]

It is not disputed that a careful analysis of actions shows us a complex machinery including intelligence, appreciation of the situation,
planning, decision, execution, and so on. Reference to the intermedi-

51 Preyer, Soziologische Theorie der Gegenwartsgesellschaft. Mitgliedschaftstheoretische Untersuchungen. on social norms, 51-54, the function of
commitments, 117-20; Soziologische Theorie der Gegenwartsgesellschaft
II. Lebenswelt – System Gesellschaft. Wiesbaden 2006, on D. Henrich,
Ethik des nuklearen Friedens. Frankfurt am Main 1990, ethics in the
nuclear epoch, 207 –10.

ated sector explains doings for an interpreter, that is, teaching about what actions are is basically the route of understanding (explaining), not only what they are, but also of features of our theoretical and practical thinking. Furthermore, the analysis of intentions, motives, will—if there is something like a "will" (mental activity)—and the moral knowledge (commitments) is essential to understand agency. In particular the exploring of the relation among the mentioned concepts leads us to a unified theory of social systems and the ascription of attitudes and actions as the elementary operation of social systems.

It is worth to mention here that action has nothing to do with our *hand* and *poesies,* that is, the craft model, but with its ascription and therefore with its fulfillment condition and ontological commitments. From the 19th century there has been a misleading tradition, not only to identify poesies and praxis, but also a misleading conception of the social and of communication, that is, the *Old European Tradition* going back to Aristotle: humans are components of the social itself who are as individuals not to resolve. The foundation of sociality is a natural teleology and not the distinction between environments of social systems. Sociality is a perfect being in general, and the intercourse is interpenetrated by law and friendship. Within this ontology it is not excluded that there are imperfect and pathological sorts of sociality. The Aristotelian universe of discourse is such that there are singularities, species (sorts), and logos (self-reference), but *not* the handling of the distinction between self-reference and reference to others. The social is an artifact. But all models of elementary interaction among present participants cannot conceptually describe the problems inherent to a complex societal system. Aristotelian ontology takes effect in Western philosophy. The assumptions of Aristotelians have blocked an adequate theory of sociality, mind, and action. The theory of complexity and contingency gives us a more fruitful framework.[52]

I dedicate this book to the memory of *Wang Jan-ming* (Wang Shou-jen) (1472-1529). His philosophical writings were a highlight of *Neo-Con-*

---

52 It is a merit of the German philosopher and sociologist N. Luhmann who has emphasized the limits of Old European tradition since the end of the sixties in principle. The theory of complexity goes back more or less to W. Weaver, Science and Complexity, American Scientist 36 1948, 536-44. The contingency approach is well-known in the theory of organization; P. R. Lawrence, J. W. Lorsch, Organization and Environment: Managing Differentiation and Integration. Boston 1967.

fucian thinking about theoretical and practical philosophy. Following Wang's unification of theoretical and practical thinking, Confucianism, Daoism, and Buddhism have the same metaphysical origin. The metaphysical ground of Daoism is *Emptiness* (xu), but also Confucianism *Saintness* refers to *Emptiness*. Buddhism talks about *Salience* (ji), but Confucianism *Saintness* refers to *Salience* also. But Confucianism is different from the way of life Daoism's. My interpretation is that Wang Jan-ming and his scholars, for example, Wang Ji, do not go along with the *Buddhist non-distinction* between "good" (friend) and "bad" (enemy) because this makes it impossible to rule the world. The *Confucian Saintness* as a distinction between these two is only indifferent toward personal affection and aversion. I became acquainted with his thoughts a long time ago by a good friend, Lee, a Chinese. He gave me lectures about Wang's thinking by which it was exemplified to me that the ascription of attitudes is born the same way in which we learn how to deal with it. On this way we are acquainted with what the preconditions for thinking and doing are and what limits of understanding come into play in our social intercourse. From my point of view the claim to rule the world is an error because the world itself cannot be dominated. World is the highest condition of complexity and contingency which is not ruled by anyone. But the *Confucian Saintness* is a theory of *vision* which we discover when observing from the borderlines and making the distinction between *inside* and *outside* and describe what happens within the two *domains of bordernization*. Just this point of view is found when we do not look for anything outside us; *we are a borderline* as Lee told me.

I want to mention in particular that Bruce Aune's sensitive comments to Part II were helpful for me to finish it.

Part I
Enigmas of Agency

1. The Reference of Action Description

*In spite of the rhetoric a Prichardian may introduce in support-
ing his theory, an impartial observer might say that, at least as
far as typical actions are concerned, Prichard's theory does not
differ a great deal from the Davidson-Sellars alternative. Both
affirm that a typical action involves both a mental, volitional
component and a physical result. The key difference is simply
that, for Prichard, the action is the mental state that has the
physical result, while for Sellars and Davidson the action is the
physical result (or upshot) of the mental state. ...
Actually, this observation is not quite correct. According to
Prichard, even a simple action of moving one's arm is an activity
with a physical result:
one brings about the relevant movement, and this requires an
activity, a 'doing' that is distinguishable from that movement.
Sellars and Davidson must reject this idea; they must say that,
although a distinction between doing and result may legitimately
be drawn in some cases—for example, in the case of bringing
about an explosion by pressing a button—there is no room
for such a distinction in simple cases of voluntary movement.
In these simple cases one's act is merely a physical movement
that, by virtue of having an appropriate mental core, is correctly
called 'an action'.*

Bruce Aune[1]

At the end of the last century the standard view on agency was dominated more or less by a Davidsonian interpretation. The leading problem
was to give an answer to the question, "What is the relation between
an agent a and an event e that brings about that the event e is an action?" The answer was that there is an event e that makes our description "something was done by x intentionally" true. Such events are
to instantiate immediately to an agent and are to individuate coarsely.
This proposal met with some critique in the past. A long time ago, the
difference among philosophers was caused by the concept of events,

---

1 B. Aune, Reason and Action. Dordrecht 1977, 23.

that is, are we committed to coarse-grained or fine-grained events in our ontology?

Firstly, I will give an analysis of what the difference between attributing and ascribing actions is. Next I will discuss A. I. Goldman's critique of the identity thesis of act and, thirdly, the role of body movements as component of actions. This leads to the problem whether the analysis of action sentences is committed to elementary events as furnishing of the universe of discourse that we suppose for our interpretation of action sentences and action description. Fourthly, I will give an answer to the question, "What sort of theory of action is possible?" A satisfactory theory of action is only given if our literal talk of the same action under different descriptions is reasoned. Davidson's view is that the logical relation between sentences is the test of the ontological commitment of the existence of entities, for example, events as presupposed entities, to understand whether or how the descriptions of actions (action sentences) have reference.

(a) Attributing and Ascribing Actions

H. L. A. Hart has argued that we use the description of actions ascriptively.[2] For him, behavior and responsibility are *defeasible concepts*. In some respect, actions are to ascribe to the responsibility of the agent. But most philosophers agree that the fundamental problem of the theory of action is the examination of act-individuation and the reference of description of action. For example, James (1) moves his finger (that causes that ...), (2) pulls the trigger, (3) fires the gun, and (4) kills Peter.

Has Peter performed *four* different acts or are these acts *one* and the *same* act? How do we interpret a description of action in the connection with the ascription of agent causation? To what extent do we bear the identity-thesis in mind?

This is the question of the nature of acts and at the same time of the ontic decision that we take into consideration. In Davidson's theory, the action of "pulling the trigger" is identical with "the killing of Peter".[3] For the identity-thesis the assumption is valid in general that if $A \equiv A'$, then it is obligatory for A to have all, and the same, properties like A'.[4]

---

2 H. L. A. Hart, The Ascription of Responsibility and Rights. Proceedings of Aristotelian Society XLIX 1949, 171-94.

3 The identity thesis goes back to Anscombe, Intention, 11, 45-6.

4 The identity symbol $\equiv$ symbolize the identity of content (G. Frege). On the

This is concluded from the logical form of action sentences and their quantificational structure. Action sentences are quantified over events and to individuate coarsely.[5]

We need to consider an answer in the sense that we can make a distinction between the ascription with the *accordion-effect*, ascription of agent causation, and the indirect instantiation of acts.

(1) James *makes happen* an event e in the sense that the *token of the event e*, just in case that the act A of e (act-token) is an *upshot*, may have a *particular causal consequence*.[6]

G.H. v. Wright, has called the event that *brought about (made happen)* an action a *result*. This was analysed in the analytical theory of action as the problem of *agent causality*, as I. Thalberg has called it.

If we make the assumption that there was a willful/intentional/ deliberate body movement, we can say in the next step:

(2) $\exists(B_i)$ $(B\ R_k\ C)$ (B is a *movement* of James's body done *intentionally i* and B *causes* that C, for example, B causes the spilling the coffee C, C causes that he surprises his wife C_1; C = C is a *causal consequence* of James's doing.)

In (2) it is relevant to distinguish between *results* and *consequences* of actions.[7] It is a *logical question* what the *result* of an action is; but *which consequences of an action will be happening* at a later time point is empirically to verify.

* The *individual event* C, like spilling the coffee, is an *upshot* of an action *a* if C is a logically necessary condition for *a*, that is, we ascribe to James that he has done *a*.

identity between the two acts A-A' Davidson, The Logical Form of Action Sentences (1967). In: Actions and Events. Oxford 1980, 109.

5 On Davidson's ontology based on the logical form of event and action sentences, for example, J. Kim, Events as Property Exemplifications. In: Supervenience and Mind. Selected Philosophical Essays. Cambridge GB 1993, 38–52, P. Pietroski, Semantics and Metaphysics of Events, 137-62. In: K. Ludwig (ed.), Davidson. Cambridge 2003.

6 G.H. v. Wright, Explanation and Understanding. Ithaca 1971, 66. Thalberg, Do we cause our own Actions?. Analysis 27 1967, 259-201.

7 The distinction goes back to Wright and is accepted extensively.

* *Upshots* in (2) are spilling the coffee and surprising the wife.
* The *events* which temporally precede the action *a* are the *causal antecedence conditions*, and
* the *events* which are temporally later are the *consequences* or *effects* of the action *a*.
* Spilling the coffee is a *consequence C* of James's moving his hand *B*, but an *upshot* of his action of bumping into the coffee cup by moving his body and surprising his wife C_I is a *consequence* of spilling the coffee *C* and *under certain conditions* it is also caused by moving his hand *B* but spilling the coffee is an *upshot*.

If someone says that James spilled the coffee to annoy his wife, Peter's action *is partially explained by the description of its cause*, his desire, want, intent, perhaps belief to annoy his wife. If someone says

* Peter has spilled the coffee *by his making happen* the bumping into the coffee cup, the spilling of the coffee *is explained as a cause* by Peter's action. In both cases the *attribution of intention* and *agency* work together.
* *Excuses* and *justifications* are characteristically for the first (redescribtion of Peter's action by desire, want, intent, belief), and *ascription of responsibility* for the second case (making happen something *x* by *y*).

But with all that we have not given any answers to the questions: *What are actions? Are actions merely body movement?* This leads us to *Davidson's view of agent-causality.*

Consequently the analysis of the relation (3) leads to the *ontological commitments of the existence-quantification* in the context of the question:

Which events show us the agency, the deeds and the doing of "James"?

If we make the assumption that in the case of *ARA'* there is a *transitive* relation, we argue:

(3) $\exists(B)$, B is a movement of James and B causes that the spilling of the coffee (intentional) = C.

The formulation of (3) is equivalent with (4)

(4) James's spilling the coffee in the sense that he *makes happen an event* e = C.

With the *accordion-effect* we give a positive interpretation of the sentence (4). This effect is limited by the agent:

(*) James spilled the coffee *unconcerned* of whether he did it willfully, intentionally, or deliberately.

We ascribe the action in all these cases, but we can evaluate and excuse such ascriptions in different ways such as, for example, James was jiggled by Henry. From Austin's and Feinberg's point of view, the *accordion-effect* is not only a *property of descriptions*, but also a *feature of actions themselves*: that is, it is not possible to describe actions that we make go on, stretch or pull together ourselves, but the actions themselves have such properties[8]: "James lifts his hand, bumps into the coffee cup, spills the coffee, and thereby surprises his wife . . ." all these is done "with one identical set of bodily movements". Feinberg argues: "Because of the accordion effect we can usually replace any ascription to a person of causal responsibility by an ascription of agency or authorship. We can, if we wish, puff out an action to include an effect, and more often than not our language obliges us by providing a relatively complex action word for the purpose. Instead of saying Smith did A (a relatively simple act) and thereby caused X in Y, we might say something of the form 'Smith X-ed Y'; instead of 'Smith open the door causing Jones to be startled', 'Smith startled Jones'".[9]

But on contrary to Austin's and Feinberg we describe what people intend to do and perform as an intentional doing. The *accordion-effect* is not a property of actions *themselves*. Not everything people do is correspondent with their intention.[10] The *accordion-effect* may show us that each consequence of a doing is a deed, but it is *not* shown *how far* the action was done intentionally. So the relationship between an intention and an intentional action or behavior is to explain.[11] *Davidson's argument is that we make a fault to assume a class of intentional actions. If*

---

8 J.L. Austin, A Plea for Excuses (1956/7), 40. In: A.L. White (ed.), The Philosophy of Action. London 1968, J. Feinberg, Action and Responsibility (1965), 106-07. In: White (ed.), The Philosophy of Action; on the accordion-effect, Davidson, Agency (1971), 61. In: Action and Events.

9 Feinberg, Action and Responsibility (1965), 106-07.

10 Davidson, Agency (1971), 45. In: Actions and Events.

11 This is accepted extensively in the philosophy of action, for example, Davidson, Agency (1971), 43-61. In: Actions and Events. Aune, Reason and Action, Mele, Springs of Action, 172-96.

this was the case, we could say of one of the same action that it was at the same time intentional and not intentional.[12]

With the descriptions (5), (6), (7) we consider *Davidson's theory* that the descriptions refer to one and the *same event*:

(5) James spills the coffee
(6) James lifts his hand, and takes his wife by surprise...
(7) James takes his wife by surprise by his doing of spilling the coffee
...

From the application of *Davidson's theory* it follows for the cases (8), (9), (10) that "James" performs only *one* movement. The statement that in all three cases

(8) the *movement* at time point z of James causes that the coffee spills
...
(9) the *movement* at time point z of James causes that he lifts the coffee cup ...
(10) the *movement* at time point z of James causes that his wife is surprised ...

encloses only *one* movement, so we conclude that the describing events of the sentences (5), (6), (7) are identical: $A \equiv A$'; there is only one and the *same event* (*identity-thesis*) that we describe in different ways. If it is the case that

(11) "Peter lifts the coffee cup intentionally" is true,

then we conclude in correspondence with Davidson's theory that the *events are actions* whose *description* could be paraphrased in common language, such as, James spills the coffee, James takes this wife by surprise, etc. Sentence (11) quantifies over linguistic entities: $\exists x$ (lifts (coffee cup, Peter x) & (x is intentional)). For x we could only put in *events*.[13]

The argument is not an empirical one, but is reasoned by the logical-syntactical form of sentences like, for example, "Peter runs deliberately, furiously, whatever, through his house in New York". Such sentences

---

12 Davidson, Agency (1971), 46. In: Actions and Events.
13 Davidson, The Individuation of Events (1969), 166. In: Action and Events.

imply "Peter runs through his house in New York". Davidson's argument is that the implication is only given if we accept *events* as particulars (individuals), that is, we have ways of stating that event-identity is true. A handling of adverbial modifications as "dressed-up predicates" is the presupposition of the application of the truth-conditional account to modifications of predicates. But the question is whether adverbial modifications like "deliberately", "intentionally", "wilfully" are *intensional* and *intentional*, ultimately making reference to the agent's mental state.

The *magna charta* of *Davidson's theory* is that such events are *particular, unrepeatable*, and *dated* events ontologically. For example, "Peter makes a phone call nervously" and "Peter makes a phone call cheerfully" are individuated by the same event that we describe differently. Therefore Davidson has argued: "If an event is an action, then under some description(s) it is primitive, and under some descriptions(s) it is intentional. This explains why we were frustrated in the attempt to assume a basic concept of agency as applied to primitive actions and extend it to further actions defined in terms of the consequences of primitive action: the attempt fails, because there are no further actions, only further descriptions."[14]

We may conclude from the sentence (11) that we go on to the sentence (12)

(12) "James lifts the coffee cup intentionally" is true to "James spills the coffee" in the sense: *he is the agent of the event*

but with (12) we do not state *act-constitutive principles*. The description of action "James spills the coffee" in (12) is different from the description in the sentence (11) in the way that we ascribe the action of "James" as an agent (agent causality). This shows that we take into account that the ascription of actions is *not* ascriptive in nature, as Hart has assumed, but also the attribution of actions does not work generally.

The "spilling the coffee" is redescribed by us in correspondence with act-constitutive principles as another action, for example, as a ritual. This is the problem of the ascription of responsibility. In the history of concepts the word "responsibility" goes back to *imputatio* (ascription).[15] We have to make the distinction between *ascription with*

---

14 Davidson, The Individuation of Events (1969), 61. In: Action and Events.
15 We find this distinction already in J. G. Darjes, Institutiones Iurispruden-

respect to different act-constitutive principles and the *event caused by agent causation.* In so far we could not conclude definitely from (12) which action was done although we ascribe agent causation with it. It is another matter if we say, "James' doings have certain consequences"; the distinction between *intrinsic* valuable actions and *extrinsic* valuable actions must be made.[16] This is not a matter of act constitutive principles itself but is to explain by the intention of an agent. But such actions are also to be characterized fulfillment-theoretically.

But how many acts are done if "James has lifted the coffee cup intentionally"? "Does the *accordion-effect* show us that the action was called intentional?"

The answer to this question has to show us what the *principle of individuation of actions* is or, on the contrary, whether this is the right question. The heart of this problem is, "What are the identity conditions of action?" "How is the theory reasoned that there is an identity between 'the pumping of James' and 'the poisoning of house occupants' in the way that 'James' does nothing but operating the pump?" In this respect we have a question of identity of acts in *ARA'*.

(b) On Critique of the Identity Theory

Goldman argues that the relation between *A-A'* has the following properties:

1. It is *asymmetrical*: if *A'* was performed by *A*, then *A* is not performed by *A'*, for example, James turns on the light by flipping the light switch, but he does not flip the light switch by turning on the light;
2. it is *irreflexive*: it is not possible that James turns on the light by turning it on;

tiae Universalis. Jena 1740. He distinguishes between *imputation iuris* and *imputation facti*. On this distinction and different sorts of responsibility, in particular in the legal system, see W. Krawietz, Risiko, Recht und normative Verantwortung. Recht und Natur. Beiträge zu Ehren von Friedrich Kaulbach. Hrsg. von V. Gerhardt, W. Krawietz. Schriften zur Rechtstheorie, Heft 153 1992, 160-172. On Hart's concept of responsibility and obligation Preyer, What a Theory of Action is possible?. Rechtstheorie 37 2006, 1-16.

16 From this distinction J. Nida-Rümelin concludes that the consequentialistic theory of action is not valid in general, Nida-Rümelin, Kritik des Konsequentialismus. München 1995, 48-50.

3. but it is *transitive*: the relation is to examine in the way that the act A' was performed by another act A.

In a given context the term *by* refers to the relationship that holds between the two acts A-A'.[17] The *by-relation* is *asymmetrical* and *irreflexive*:

* if James did A *by* doing of B, then it is false:

1. that James did b *by* the doing of A
   and
2. that James did A *by* the doing of A.

A possible answer could be: James's particular act may be called by us "his relational property": "the killing of..." can cause "the firing of the gun". This is strange talk because we tend *to confuse the causal relation between events with the explanatory relation between statements*. The *fact* that the gun has fired is not to explain *causally* by the *fact* that James has killed Peter. The action that James performed by his doing has brought about Peter's death—we describe it as "the killing of Peter"—, and it may be caused by "the firing of the gun":

* James's act of killing Peter is the very *activity* which *caused* that Peter died, and this *activity* may be of such a kind that it has *caused* the pulling of the trigger.[18]

It is useful to make the distinction between *action* and *activity*. *Action* is a technical notion; *activities*, such as gardening, walking, teaching, thinking etc. is a *word for concepts in our ordinary life*.

When we describe an action, for example, "the killing of Peter by James", a reference to "Peter" must be involved if we describe the action of "James". But the death of "Peter" was *no* part of "James's"

17 Goldman, Theory of Human Action, 5, 1–10.
18 See Shwayder, The Stratification of Behavior. A System of Definitions Propounded and Defined. London 1965, 31-2. Have in mind H.A. Prichard's-view: "An action, i.e. a human action, instead of being the originating or causing of some change, is an activity of willing some change, this usually causing some change, and in some cases a physical change, its doing or not doing this depending on the physical conditions of which the agent is largely ignorant", Prichard, Acting, Willing, Desiring". In: A.L. White (ed.), The Philosophy of Action, London 1968, 65.

doing like raising his arm, moving his fingers, pulling the trigger, firing the gun, and so on. Peter's death was a causal consequence of his art and not a part of it, that is, of the action that was done by James: "James shot Peter dead" and the consequence was that his friend died. When describing the doing of James it may be that the description was stretched and pulled and we refer to the "death of Peter". But stretching and pulling together is not a property of any act itself. James's act is to describe as an activity, and Peter's death was an upshot of this doing but no part of this act. An action and its causal consequences are to characterize as two distinct items. The significant point is that the relation in *ARA'* is not a matter between *acts* but between *results* of acts, which is to explain.

But there is just another point for analyzing the *by-relation*. If we use singular terms to specify the relationship of relevant acts, we could not say meaningfully:

(1) James turns on the light *by* James's flipping the switch.

The word *by* is not a clear example to characterize a relation.[19] It can be used to connect the two sentences:

(2) James turns on the light *by* flipping the switch.

We read this statement in the sense:

(3) James flips the switch and *thereby* he turns on the light.

H.A. Prichard has analyzed this reading as:

(4) James caused: the switch was flipped, and *thereby* he caused the turning on of the light.[20]

The *agent causality* would this way be reduced to a *causality of ends*:

19 On the meaning of *by* J. Hornsby, Actions. London 1980, 6-8, 27-8, Kim, Noncausal Connections, 24-28. In: Supervenience and Mind: on the *by-relation* (generation), Aune, Reason and Action, 15-16.

20 H.A. Prichard, Action, Willing, Desiring, 59-69. In: Moral Obligations. Oxford 1949; on Prichard, see A.I. Melden, Willing (1960), 75-77. In: White (ed.), Philosophy of Action.

(5) ∃A (A is an *activity* by James with respect to the *fact* that A causes the flipping of the switch and *thereby* causes the turning on of the light).

The word *thereby* may connote a *by-relation* in these statements, but in the given reading the relation does not hold between *acts* but between *upshots of acts*. The event of the flipping of the switch therefore causes the event of turning on the light. The act or the activity of the first event may then hold in a transitive relation or causation respectively to the second event, but this interpretation of "James turns on the light by flipping the switch" is identical with his act of turning on the light. The problem of the relationship between both events leads us back to the *identity-theory*. We look for an event that both events make true. It is to explain how something that is "true" of an action would be also "true" of any other event.

(c) Actions and Body Movements

We have argued that the statements of the sentences (8), (9), (10) are about only *one* movement and therefore the described events in the sentences (5), (6), (7) are identical.

Are actions (agency) nothing but movements of the body as *primitive* actions[21]?

If we make the assumption that there is a cardinal dependency to characterize primitive actions in the following way: the doing of "James" x is a *primitive* action if and only if

1. x is a *primitive* action and
2. if "James" performs x, then there is no other action y that is performed by x in the sense that x is caused by y.

So we conclude from this dependency: every action of "James" is either a *primitive action* or *another event* in a causal chain under a certain description, and some earlier links in the chain are also to describe as actions performed by him. If "James", for example, "moves his finger", "turns on the light switch", "switches on the light", "lights up the room", we could describe his body movements as different actions, and every action is the cause of the one that follows. The general problem

21 Davidson, Agency (1971), 59. In: Actions and Events.

of individuating action, that is, the reference of description, lies in this proposal: if we redescribe the series from "moving the hand" to "lighting up the room" as a singular action in a chain of more or less direct effects, then the descriptions like, for example, "moving the finger", "switching on the light", "lighting up the room" denote causal relations between events, but none of these items is a description of an action. If we demand to specify the descriptions and properties to primitive actions, then it is to conclude that all instances that satisfy a singular term are to classify as primitive actions, but others are not.

However, in an object language describing items of behavior we cannot determine whether a certain description of an action is a description of a primitive action or not. If James, for example, raises his right arm, so the "raising of his right arm now" may, for some observers, be a basic description of James's action. But James can raise his right arm by his left arm also if, for example, his right arm lies in a loop. In this case "James raises his arm" specifies an action, but the description is not one of a primitive action. If something is right with the concept of primitive action, we could expect to find a basic description of any particular action of "James", but we do not expect that an exemplification of a basic description like, for example, "James moves his finger" describes action.

What *reclassification* is to put forward on the status of body movements like "contracting the muscles", also as a causal factor, and the physiological process?

We could make the assumption that the body movement that happens if, for example, a fist is clenched, is closing the fingers. The later movement is a result of another movement that was before it and we can disregard it. The analysis of the role of the body and muscle movements in action theory shows us two properties:

1. If we begin with the assumption that body movements are dependent components of actions, the analysis of muscle contraction of "clenching the fist" does not lead to the conclusion that an action begins before the fingers are closed, namely at the time point of "bracing the muscles". The temporally earlier events, and also the prior items of behavior and body movements, are ultimately unknown, and they are to compare, for example, with the discovering of an initiated movement of throwing a ball.

2. But do we conclude from body movements as dependent components that someone who "is clenching his fist" is *doing* "the bracing of his muscles"?

I do not think that this is the case. If the context within the body movements is to describe as action that has changed, then the same movements are an action no longer. It is an empirical question which act was performed while the muscles were braced. Whatever may be the case, the contraction happens, but such an event is not brought about. Therefore we conclude: whatever role the physiological process may play, such events are to distinguish from our reasons for action.[22]

Certainly we know that no one moves her finger unless her finger moves; and we know that we can tell by observation what people do, and that we could not observe someone move her finger unless we saw her finger move. But we also know that these considerations alone could not suffice to show that her finger's moving is a part of her action—no more than similar considerations could suffice to show that Jones's death was a part of Smith's killing him. Again we know that it is typical of an agent that when there is an action she moves her body and thereby initiates a series of events so that something she wants comes to happen. But this consideration does not circumscribe an action beyond showing it to be where the agent is. It is not at all clear what would definitively settle the question as to which things are parts of an action. This will not seem to be worrying if we are aware that there need not be any more plain truths about the events that are actions than there are plain truths about action (about agency, and things people do). *So now we know what the essential problem of a theory of action is that claims to individuate actions as events by movements of our body or to attribute actions in the framework of a basic ontology of events.*

In sum: We do not use action sentences in an exclusively *ascriptive* way, but we could use these sentences *ascriptively* as well as *descriptively*. If we individuate doings as events, we ask for the attribution of action as a particular event which has caused something. The individuation of events as actions means that we attribute doings *directly* to the agent. Therefore *defeasibility* does not work when ascribing actions in essential On the contrary: if we ascribe responsibility, the ascription has contextual features. Shwayder has argued that a *presumption of success* and *success* in action is a *defeasible* concept.[23] I have no problem with this distinction. In the contemporary debate between Minimal Semantics and Radical Pragmatics, F. Recanati turn is: "A distinguishing

---

22 On the role of body movements, the robust substrate of actions, see also Wright, Normen, Werte und Handlungen. Frankfurt am Main 1994, 231-33, 241-43.

23 Shwayder, The Stratification of Behaviour, 121.

characteristic of pragmatic interpretation is its defeasibility. The best explanation we can offer for an action given the available evidence may be revised in the light of new evidence. Even if an excellent explanation is available, it can always be overridden if enough new evidence is adduced to account for the subject's behavior. It follows that any piece of evidence may turn out to be relevant for the interpretation of an action. In other words, there is no limit to the amount of contextual information that can affect pragmatic interpretation".[24] If this were true, then no semantic analysis of action sentences would be possible. I have no doubts that Recanati's contextualism is going wrong.

Ascriptive sentences are not wholly theoretical or factual, but their use shows us a feature of our own discretion and estimation.[25] The expressions "Peter did x" and "Peter is responsible for x" do not mean the same because the "doing a" asks for agent causality and the ascription of responsibility presupposes contexts, value orientations, social norms, and so on, that is, act-constitutive principles. It is obvious, for example, that the use of "obliged" is dependent on "being obliged by something". The two uses of being obliged (Hart: being obliged and having or being under an obligation) and their applications to the ascription of actions do not distinguish far enough between actions that are *undertaken* and deeds that are *done*.[26] With the consideration of this distinction we can make a difference between the responsibility for an action and the responsibility for an action I have done.

(d) What Sort of Theory of Action is possible?

Following N. Rescher, Goldman analyzes the individuation of acts with the principal distinction between both:

1. Act-*types*: the act-properties like "running", "killing", "holding a lecture" and so on. If we ascribe an act to an agent, then we exemplify an act property.
2. Act-*token*: the performance of an act like holding a lecture at a given time point.[27]

24 F. Recanati, Literal Meaning. Cambridge 2004, 54.
25 This is emphasized by Feinberg, Action and Responsibility (1965), 116.
26 On Hart's distinction Preyer, What a Theory of Action is Possible?. Rechtstheorie 4 2006, 436-38.
27 N. Rescher, Aspects of Action, 85. In: The Logic of Decision and Action.

An *act-token* is not a property, but an exemplification of an *act-type* by an agent at a given time-point. So the natural way to individuate *act-tokens* is: two act-tokens are identical if and only if they were exemplified by the same agent, the same property, and the same time-point. Goldman does not assert that Davidson's identity-thesis is irrelevant.[28] From his point of view, it is a requirement to find identity-conditions of actions to give an answer to the question:

What do we mean to say with statements about *act-types*?

For this purpose, Goldman makes the distinction between a*ct-types* and *act-tokens*:

> The heart of my position is that act-token *A* and act-token *A'* are identical only if they are tokens of the same type (property). But since killing Smith and moving one's finger are distinct types, John's killing Smith (at *t*) and John's moving his finger (at *t*) are distinct act-tokens.[29]

Statements about *act-types* mean:

> (When) we say ‚John signaled for a turn' … we ascribe an act property or (what is to say the same thing) act type to John: the property of signaling for a turn .. To ascribe an act type to someone is to say that he exemplified it. If John and Oscar perform the same act (i.e. do the same thing), they exemplify the same act type.[30]

The semantic content of action sentences are *types* (properties), and we use these sentences to ascribe these properties by a *nominalization* of this content.

> Since an act token is standardly designated by a nominalized form of action sentence and since an action sentence associated with such a nominalization asserts that a person exemplifies a certain act property, it is natural to view the designatum of such a nominalization as an exemplifying of an act property by a person. Thus John's (signaling for a turn) is an exemplifying by John of the property of (signaling for a turn).[31]

Edited by N. Rescher. Pittburg 1967, Goldman, A Theory of Human Action, 10-19.

28 On the reconstruction of the identity theses Goldman, A Theory of Human Action, 37-38.

29 Goldman, A Theory of Human Action, 11.

30 Goldman, The Individuation of Action. Journal of Philosophy LXVIII 1971, 769.

31 Goldman, The Individuation of Action (1971), 770.

From this account, Goldman takes the theoretical step leading to the assertion that thesis expressions designate events that we distinguish as *act-types*:

> Moreover, since the act type of (signalling for a turn) is distinct from the act type of (extending his arm out of the car window), it seems natural to say that (John's exemplifying of the act type of (signalling for a turn) is distinct from (John's) exemplifying of the act type of (extending his arm out of the car window.[32]

For Goldman, action sentences designate *act-tokens* by their nominalized form, and their truth is to verify by the reference to such tokens. Without any theoretical risk he can make the assumption that the expressions

(1) "I did the same that you did" and
(2) "he did the same that you did"

do not require the *identity of particular events*. For his theory, the talk of

(3) bringing about a movement,
(4) bringing about the movement of my hand,
(5) causing the attentiveness of the waiter

exemplifies three distinct *act-properties* (types). But none of these properties are one and the same action.

How far do the nominalization of action sentences designate act-tokens? Is it the case that action sentences are true by virtue of their specification to particular actions?

Goldman's universal quantification said:

* The *act-type* of giving a sign is to distinguish from the *act-type* of moving the hand.

Normally we would make the assumption that any exemplification of the act-type of giving a sign is different from every exemplification of the *act-type* of moving the hand. But the quantification is presumably not valid without a particular context-reference. J. Hornsby has argued

---

32 Goldman, The Individuation of Action (1971), 771, on this point in particular, see Hornsby, Actions, 16-19.

correctly that it is possible for us to have reasons to say that the property of being an "author of a book" is different from the property of being an "author of an article", and these properties are to distinguish from other properties of a person. If someone has a particular property it is different from his particular other properties. If we suppose, for example, that

* "... is an *exemplification* of James's property ..."
and
* "... *has* the property ..."

play the *same logical role*, so the argument about the authorship picks out the same role that is necessary for Goldman's theory. But on the basis of this *argument about authorship* we could conclude that Goldman is not Goldman, Hornsby argues.[33]

> Goldman's neglect of the generality in action sentences is manifest in his argument itself. At the end of the quoted passage, he concludes that John's exemplifying of the property of signaling for a turn is distinct from John's exemplifying of the property of extending the arm. 'What exemplifyings by John are these?' Do we not need to know which particulars are in question in order to tell whether distinct particulars are in question? It is true that, so far as Goldman is concerned, it is not going to matter which particular actions he means to speak of, because he thinks that whichever exemplifying by John of signaling for a turn it is, it will be distinct form any exemplifying by John of extending the arm. But if he thinks that, then it is a general conclusion for which he should argue.[34]

Hornsby argues that it is not required that Goldman settles his general claim which "particular particulars".

What sort of *theory of action is possible* when we suppose the individuation of acts as an explanandum of the theory of action?

If Goldman develops his theory of action under the feature of *individuating acts*, then the same questions as in the ontology of events proposal arise. In a strict sense no theory of action is possible. But there is a theory that corresponds to the theory of action. Let us call that a theory of agent. Its theme is not simply a rational individual agent like Davidson agues, but agents within a social frame of reference, and we

---

33 Hornsby, Actions, 18.
34 Hornsby, Actions, 17, 17-19. Hornsby refers to Goldman, The Individuation of Action (1971), 771.

suppose acts they perform. One may call such *agents rational* if their behavior is made intelligible, that is, if we can ascribe *epistemic attitudes* and apply the *act-constitutive principle* to them. And this is the task of re-interpretation. A different feature of this theory is that the analysandum consists of *act-predicates* (as classificatory expressions) and their *ascription*, whereas, in contrast to that, a theory of action asks for the *individuation of acts* and the *reference of singular terms* (action sentences, — description as singular terms). Instead of

* James slaps Peter and Mary is angry

the *theory of agent* makes the assumption:

* that Mary is angry *because* James slaps Peter.[35]

An alternative account of Goldman's proposal is:

* If a person does A, then we assume that the same person *thereby* performs A(A') with respect to *different types of primary reasons*.

From here it follows that we analyze the ascription of actions on the main connecting thread from epistemic attitudes that are connected with the network of attitudes.

The *theory of agent* is to introduce as a theory not only of translation but also of re-interpretation because there are no requirements of counterparts to it in a plausible theory of action. On the other hand, we might expect such counterparts like, for example, (12) "James lifts the coffee cup intentionally" is true we may infer "James spills the coffee" in the sense: he is the agent of the event[36] as the corresponding counterpart of the theory of action to the theory of agent. If Goldman asserts that the act of "signaling in traffic" is generated by the different act of "raising the arm", then, Prichard would argue that signaling is determined by the act of moving the arm. If we make the assumption that there are corresponding counterparts between a theory of agent and the theory of action in Goldman's sense, then the instantiation of acts is *indirect* in principle. For him, the concept of generation instantiates acts directly. In correspondence with his argument, the ascription of action makes the assumption:

35 On the analysis of *because* I 2. (d), in this book.
36 See I 1. (a), in this book.

* If an agent is extending his arm in a certain way, then he is signaling a coming turn *because* in a specific domain there is an interconnection between both.

For all ascriptions of action there is the requirement of satisfaction of contextual presuppositions that take effect in the analysis of the word "because" in sentences like "...did...because...". I call this the principle of *constitution of instantiation* of act-tokens. So we explain agent causation in the following way:

* If James fires a torpedo and the Bismarck goes down *because* he fires the torpedo, then he sends the Bismarck to the bottom of the sea.

However, if James had done this as an actor in a movie we would not say that he sent the ship down because what happened has a particular contextual presupposition. This account corresponds surely to Goldman's principle of causal generation.

If we begin to describe items of behavior in continuation as an action, our description is essentially incomplete, and it is always an uncertainty to fix the positive values of such descriptions definitely, such is, the ends and doings are not determined under certain conditions. We are confronted with the *incompleteness* of such descriptions. The best principle to limit these descriptions is the propositional expression, that is, it is the case that ... In this sense we can apply the *accordion-effect* to the descriptions of actions: each sequence squeezed down to a minimum or stretched out gives us a deed. We describe actions if we give an answer to the question, "What was done?", and we ascribe actions if we ask for the act-constitutive principle of the doing of different sorts. If the ascription of actions takes off from its redescription, an interpreter assumes for its ascription:

* x believes that a for z in y is required to reach his goal or certain effects.

To form an intention is also a matter of our beliefs, and we interpret *shall* as an expression of an attitude. Beliefs, desires, and other intentional attitudes play a relevant role in common explanation of intentional behavior. *But intention is distinct from belief because it plays another role in the explaining of intentional behavior.* Therefore we interpret *willing* as a particular form of *intending* that involves the conception of bringing about a certain effect and also upshots as expected consequences.[37] The *motivational strength* is a particular problem. Intention itself does not explain it.

2. Explaining Action

(a) Theoretical and Practical Thinking

> *Knowledge acquired through personal realization is different form that acquired through listening to discussion.*
>
> Wang Yan-ming

Many philosophers would agree that one must distinguish between *deliberation, justification*, and *explanation*.[38] In deliberation we ask for the course of action before we do something. In explanation we do not ask for what is right or wrong but only what motivated the agent, like 'my, your, our ... reason for doing...'". In justification we ask for the best course after acting. Usually a distinction is made between theoretical and practical thinking. We exemplify theoretical thinking by assertions and practical thinking by intentions.[39] To every propositional content $*p*$ there is a negation $*$non-$p*$ as a result of the negation of $*p*$, which we call negation. The $*$ symbolizes the non-nominalized propositional content of "p": $*p*$. If we assert the propositional content $*$non-$p*$, we call that *Verneinung* (Frege). It is an assertive affirmation of the negation of a propositional content which is a propositional content that is negative to another propositional content. The *Verneinung*, which is itself an affirmation, is opposed to another affirmation.[40] Sentences like 'I shall do x' are not an assertion, nor are they predictions, but they are sentences

---

37 W. Sellars, Thought and Action, 108-9. In: K. Lehrer (ed.), Freedom and Determinism. New York 1966.

38 K. Baier, The Moral Point of View. A rational Basis of Ethics. New York 1958, 40-50.

39 Theoretical sentences are assertoric sentences and practical sentences are imperative -, intention and optative sentences.

40 The analysis of *Verneinung* goes back to G. Frege, Logische Untersuchungen (Der Gedanke (1918), Die Verneinung (1918), Gedankengefüge (1923)). Zweiter Teil: Die Verneinung, In: Kleine Schriften, Zweite Auflage. Hrsg. und mit Nachbemerkung zur Neuauflage versehen von I. Angelelli, Hildeshim 1990, 362-78. This is accepted among many semanticists, see also E. Tugendhat, Vorlesungen zur Einführung in die sprachanalytische Philosophie. Frankfurt am Main 1976, 66-68. A gen-

with which we express an intention (intention-sentence). We can deny intention-sentences like assertions. The negation of such sentences "I shall do x" is not an error but that the speaker (agent) has not fulfilled (realized) an intention. This is not disputed among many philosophers. The consciousness of action implies at the same time that we can also leave something be, and therefore we deliberate about, 'What is to do or not?' All deliberations go along with a *question* like, "Is it true or to fulfill that...?", "What shall (will) I (you, we, they) do?" or, "Which course of action is the best to take for me, for us or for him?".

But is practical thinking original, or is it an illusion?

Davidson argues that it is "practical only in the subject, not in the issue".[41] *Practical thinking is a illusion because practical thinking itself does not cause any action.* He introduces the principle of continence, that is, to perform the action judged best on the basis of all available relevant reasons.[42] Such judgments are formed by *all things considered judgments* as a special case of a *prima facie judgment* in respect to all relevant properties of the action known by the agent. *Prima facie judgments* are like "Something is in so far x as it is y"; for example, the car is useful as I can drive quickly to my shop, it weighs upon my mind as it is too expensive, it pleases me because my neighbor is envious of me, and so on. Davidson's theory of judgment is near a stoic theory of judgment. *Prima facie judgments* are "Judgments that actions are desirable in so far they have a certain attribute".[43] But it is an illusion that such thinking leads to an action as a consequence of a deliberation as such. Every choice (preference) is a judgment in this tradition, a *prohairesis krisis estin*.[44] But for *prima facie judgments* it is, for him, the form of the *statement* and not the judgment itself.[45] There is a distinction between response and judgment. If we have classificatory concepts, then judgments are to be built: this is a lion, this is green etc., which are true or false.

The *new problem* of practical reasoning is that such reasons are not

eral analysis of structures of propositional content is given by different fulfillment conditions, Preyer, Donald Davidson's Philosophy, 291-97.

41 Davidson, How is Weakness of the Will Possible (1970), 39. In: Action and Events.

42 Davidson, How is Weakness of the Will Possible (1970), 41. In: Action and Events.

43 Davidson, Intending (1978), 98. In: Action and Events.

44 J. Nida-Rümelin, Über menschliche Freiheit. Stuttgart 2005 has recalled this tradition.

45 Davidson, Intending (1977), 97, note 7. In: Action and Events.

detached conclusions from what is better or desirable from the agent's point of view. Therefore an *all things considered judgment*—that is, the agent takes into his deliberations all relevant properties of an action for his decision—, is to continue to an *all-out* or *unconditional judgment* as an imperative *This action is desirable.*[46] The desirable property of an action may be a reason for an action, but it is not a sufficient condition. For Davidson, practical thinking is an illusion because it is only a requirement for thinking about what is to do and this deliberation has an action as its consequence. Therefore the transition from an *all things considered judgment* to an *all-out judgment* shows the *illusion of practical thinking*: it is not a matter of our free thinking but of our mental states whether we listen to the voice of reason. This shows the *weakness of the will*. It is not the case that will-weaked people act against an *all-out judgment*. This is not possible. But they have a weak will because their *all-out judgment* is incoherent with their *all things considered judgment*. Therefore, weakness of the will shows us the *illusion of practical thinking*. The agent has reasons for his action, but his reasons are not the best.

It seems that pure intending is a particular case of unfulfilled intentions, but *the subject is intending in general*, that is, "intending abstracted from a context which may include any degree of deliberation and any degree of success in execution"[47]; that is, we have to abstract something to grasp what intending is. Therefore the analysis of pure intending re-interprets practical thinking in a particular way and gives it another turn because the relationship between intention and intentional action is to explain by *pure intending* as a subclass of all-out judgments as a kind of intending that occurs without practical reasoning, action, or consequences and directed to actions of the agent.[48] Davidson has reaffirmed his proposal of practical thinking and incontinence: "I am committed to the view that an agent is incontinent only if he fails to reason from a conditional 'all things considered judgment' that a certain course of action is best to the unconditional conclusion that course of action is best."[49] The problem here is that Davidson has noted *how*

---

46 See also I 2. (ii), II 1., in this book.
47 Davidson, Intending (1977), 89. In: Action and Events.
48 Davidson, Intending (1977), 83-102. In: Action and Events.
49 Davidson, Replies to Essays I-IX, 206. In: B. Vermazen, M. Hintikka (eds.), Essays on Davidson: Actions and Events. Oxford 1985, see also Mele, Philosophy of Action, 77-79. In: K. Ludwig (ed.), Donald Davidson. Cambridge 2003.

people make the virtue of continence their own and he thinks such behavior is not any more difficult that being brave. This leads us to the problem of the *strength of motivation* of doing something or not. Practical thinking does not take any effect in our acting by itself. It is dependent on the strength of our desire of the flesh, customs, training, the disposition to listen to the voice of reasoning, and so on. Incontinent actions are an error in a set of the most part true beliefs and an evidence that practical thinking is not original.[50] *Therefore an answer to the question of the origin of practical thoughts must be given.*

Theoretical and practical thinking is not completely distinct. But at the same time practical thinking is to rehabilitate partially. It is not totally illusionary because the *practical judgment has a direct relevance to an action.* Practical knowledge has a cognitive content that is expressed in notions of knowledge in general.

Such knowledge is not only a skill and a disposition of practical thought, but also a matter of practical consistency, that is, the agent is committed by itself and its deliberation. Only people who are *self-conscious*, that is, conscious of themselves as thinker (speaker, agent) dispose about this principle. *Self-knowledge and the understanding of others like ourselves is the key to distinguishing between behavior and intentional behavior as intentional.*[51] Self-reference (first person thinking) takes the relationship between first- and second-order intentional states into consideration. In the folk psychological framework we assume that there is a reciprocal assumption that agents are authoritative about their self-reference. But we assume that there are common thoughts under certain conditions where it is included that the members of a social system who apply the *social frame of reference* have the capacity to locate stimuli in the environment they perceive. The individuation condition implies an indexical component, an objective component, and sortals.[52] With these we identify situations (entities of awareness). The ascription of attitudes and the explaining of action are not independent of such a frame of reference. From my point view it is the reason why the distinction between intentional and non-intentional

---

50 On *incontinence*, see II 2., in this book.

51 Mele, Springs of Action, 42, has emphasized this; see also C. Taylor, *Human Agency and Language.* Cambridge 1985.

52 E. Tugendhat, Vorlesungen zur Einführung in die sprachanalytische Philosophie. Frankfurt am Main 1976, 25. *Vorlesung:* Der Mechanismus der raumzeitlichen Identifizierung und die Konstitution des Gegenstandbezuges, 426-39.

requires the application of intentional notions, and this is the difference to the framework of neuroscience.

Often the thinker (speaker, agent) does not have an explicit knowledge of the application of the distinction between intentional and non-intentional. This requires conceptual resources which incorporate propositional attitudes in learning and teaching of mental and social predicates. Therefore mental and social concepts have to figure *as* mental and *as* social. Therefore an elucidation (explanation) and teaching of it is required. This will become clear if we think about the moving force of practical thinking. We take a step towards a unified theory of thought, meaning and action if we analyze the relationship between moral knowledge as a form of practical thinking in a situation where we learn how to plan actions and are acquainted with principles and their applications. *Self-consciousness or self-reference involves reference to others as a distinction; we mark the borderlines between I/we and you/they (others)*. Therefore the ascription of attitudes is connected with the social frame of reference. If we learn how to plan actions, to make a distinction between I/we and you/we (others), and the application of principles, we learn at the same time how to do something, and how to do it together. In these cases the content of thoughts of myself and others we perceive/describe/identify/re-identify is presupposed in our doings. Just this shows us that moral knowledge and the different sorts of virtues play together.

What bridges the internal-external differentiation between thoughts, situations of doing, and their environment?

Teaching what beliefs and intentions are connected with the learning of conceptual distinctions and also with moral predicates. But here we find also the place where we are acquainted with conative attitudes like, for example, seeing something as beautiful. We are not only a plaything of our dispositions, we can deliberate about our actions in respect of different features. This leads me to a principle of decision, the principle of exclusionary reasons[53] and to the question whether practical thinking has a result that leads to a correspondent action. The agent comes to a judgment with a direct relevance of an action and believes that he reaches a certain goal by doing what follows from his deliberation.

Epistemologically there are internal and external relationships which are to distinguish. We attend to the thought standing alone as externally outside us, like a Fregean Thought, and, metaphorically speaking, as an internal relation in the mind. The philosophical problem is how to

53 See II 2., in this book.

explain the plausibility of the latter. The relation is not logically necessary. The *social frame of reference* which is externally placed in the
epistemic differentiation of the social systems (social universe) takes
effects in our explanation and ascription of attitudes. It is the thinker's
(speaker's, agent's) knowledge of its position and employment within its
environment. The epistemic qualification takes effect within the social
frame of ascription. The counterfactual example of the ascription of
beliefs about arthritis shows that we would not ascribe the speaker a
true belief, we would not revise him because there is a linguistic com-
munity and there are linguistic and epistemic authorities. The anti-indi-
vidualistic argument in the philosophy of the mental shows that there
is no ultimate (constitutive) epistemic authority. This is a critique of the
elimination of referential opacity by the truth-centered theory of radical
interpretation because the epistemic attitudes limit physical externalism of individuation of attitudinal content by causal relations that we
are aware of directly in our environment.[54] The riddle of attitudes is
their lingual expressions because we have no problem of understanding
meaning without a linguistic representation. Lingual expression gives
us oblique context (semantic opacity) only.

The epistemic first person view is to harmonize with externalism partially when we change our perspective. It is not a problem to assume or
find a Cartesian *faculty* as epistemic basis via introspection, nor is it a
Davidsonian *behavioral basic* issue of the individuation of attitudinal
content in triangulation, and neither a radical behavioristic explanation
of the mental by merely behavioral items. The intentional own states
and also sensations have two components that lead us to the semantics
of mental predicates in the first and third person attitude as a re-interpretation of the role of folk psychology and its limits. The individuation
condition is to re-interpret from this point of view.

---

54 On Davidson's externalism of triangulation Preyer, Donald Davidson's
Philosophy, 34-40, 75-80

(b) Belief and Intention

> I take it as obvious that linguistic behavior is
> intentional and so requires belief. It is only where
> intention and belief are present that the concept
> of a mistake can be applied.
>
> D. Davidson[55]

Riddles emerge if we begin to describe given behavior as action:

What refers to our description of behavior if we redescribe it as an action? Was my stumbling over the carpet an act that I have performed? Was the thief who crept along to my house warned by my switching on the light? Was my warning an action that is to ascribe to myself?

What I intend and do is described by us as intentional action, but not all of my intentional doings correspond with my prior intentions.[56]

What are intentions, beliefs, and desires? How does their interplay cause an action?

Davidson's *syncategorematic* account of intention, "the intention with which James went to church", is that this expression does not state or refer to anything because there are not such states on intending, there are only intentional actions.[57] It is worthwhile to analyze his *first proposal of 1963* because it was the renaissance of the causal explanation of action in a time that was partially dominated by the *logical connection argument* and Wittgenstein's and Ryle's philosophy. His causal explanation by primary reasons was a critique of an intentional explanation (logical connection argument) and takes effect in the analytical theory of action. At the same time he gives a particular answer to the roles of laws for the explanation of action. In the following it is to show that, on the contrary, intentions link beliefs and other pro attitudes (primary reasons) and actions. I call that the *problem of intention*.

"James" is the agent of an event, if and only if there is a description of what he has done that makes a sentence true, and this sentence states that "James" did something intentionally. In accordance with this theory, the statement that "James" did something intentionally has a particular fulfillment condition that we analyze semantically on the

---

55 Davidson, Problems of the Explanation of Action (1987), 116. In: Problems of Rationality.

56 Anscombe, Intention, 31 was the first to formulate this problem.

57 Davidson, Action, Reason, and Causes (1963), 3-4. In: Action and Events.

sentential level. The claim that an agent does something intentionally is to redescribe in the following way by *primary reasons*:

(*) The act of doing something intentionally is caused by primary reasons, that is, by a complex mental state. Such states are composed of

1. pro attitudes toward an action *a* with a particular property *p* that we express in prima face judgments, and
2. the belief that this action *a* has, under a given description, the desirable property *p*.

Examples for pro attitudes are desires, economic preferences, aesthetic evaluations, social conventions, and private and public goal orientations, which reveal attitudes of an agent toward actions. Therefore these are original mental states or dispositions. But the pro-attitudes are not events or episodes or anything else that "James" intends. Therefore, "To know a primary reason why someone acted as he did to know an intention with which the action was done".[58] This is Davidson's version of the desire-belief account.

Explaining actions by primary reason is a critique of the intentionalists' proposal. In sum:

1. Knowing the intention does not mean to know the *cause*, and therefore the primary reason in detail, for example, if someone knew my intention of visiting my mother's friend in hospital; one does not know whether I do my duty only, or whether I take it as a chance to buy a new suit in the shop near the hospital, and so on.
2. Descriptions of intended results of behavior could give us a better explanation of actions as intentions themselves: "...than stating that the result was intended or desired. 'It will soothe your nerves' since the first in the context of explanation implies the second; but the first does better because if it is true, the facts will justify my choice of action".[59]
3. The logical connection argument gives us no analysis of the word *because* in sentences "He did it because...". Thereby we attribute and name details about desires and beliefs to an agent.[60]

---

58 Davidson, Action, Reasons, and Causes (1963), 7. In: Action and Events.
59 Davidson, Action, Reasons, and Causes (1963), 8. In: Action and Events.
60 Davidson, Action, Reasons, and Causes (1963), 11. In: Action and

But do directed intentions of future action build on the agent's beliefs?

This leads to *pure intending* in difference to intention and intentional action as the foundation for our explaining action as a modified version of the desire-belief thesis.[61] It claims to show us how intending and intentional action are connected. This is a modification of his earlier account of *action with an intention*. Pure intending is a kind of intending that occurs without practical reasoning, action, or consequences. It is possible that I intend to go to the movies this evening, but I have not decided to do it, deliberated about it, formed an intention, and so on. But it might happen that, despite my intention, I do not do so nor even try to do so. Intending of this kind is a problem if we claim to analyze the concept of intention without mysterious acts of the will or other sorts of causation that are not usual in science.

The *Davidson-view* gives us a hint to answer these questions: "To intend to perform an action is, on my account, to hold that it is desirable to perform an action of a certain sort in the light of what one believes is and will be the case. But if one believes no such action is possible, then there can be no judgment that such an action consistent with one's belief is desirable. There can be no such intention."[62] To answer the relationship among intending to act, acting with an intention and acting intentionally (intentional action), Davidson introduces, in contrast to prima facie judgments, so-called all-out (unconditional, unrestricted) judgments like *this action is desirable*.[63] The *semantic content of desirability* is to take in the explanation of action. Prima facie judgments cannot be connected directly to actions because they tell us nothing about whether the action ought to be done. The fact that something is prima facie right or wrong does not imply the desirability of the action.[64] Therefore, an all-out judgment is to introduce by which we decide on the desirable property of an action as a sufficient reason to do something or not. This judgment takes into play all my reasons: *it is the intention*.[65] This judgment stops conditional judgments; they

Events. This is modified in: Davidson, Paradoxes of Irrationality (1982), 173. In: Problems of Rationality.

61 Davidson, Intending (1978), 83-102. In: Actions and Events.

62 Davidson, Intending (1978), 101-01. In: Action and Events.

63 On the *desirability-axiom* with reference to Ramsey and Jeffrey's system, Davidson, A Unified Theory of Thought, Meaning, and Action (1980), 161-64. In: Problems of Rationality.

64 Davidson, Intending (1978), 37. In: Action and Events.

65 Davidson, Intending (1978), 101. In: Action and Events. In the case of

are practical only in the *subject* but not in the *issue*.[66] But this does not exclude that the action was a weak-willed one because the agent does not have enough virtue.

The *Davidson-view* assimilates intentions to beliefs (unconditional judgments). The result of this theory of action is: in order to understand an action with an intention we require pro attitudes, beliefs and the primitive action itself. The analysis of the causal relations of these components has to be added to it. Davidson argues that, if an ontological reduction to events as our basic ontology is placed at our disposal—the ontic decision of individual events—, it "is enough to answer many puzzles about the relation between the mind and the body, and to explain the possibility of autonomous action in the world of causality".[67] He argues: an agent who moves his hand brings about a movement; *he is directly the agent of the event*. Hence someone is the agent of an event if there is a description of his doing that makes the sentence "true", saying that it was an intentional action. The statement "James brings about something" has two different readings:

1. James does something *a* that causes *c*, or
2. James is the agent.

"*x* brings about *c*" usually means: *x* does something *a* that brings about *c*, such as, he pours gas onto the ground, and lights it with the result: (that) there is a fire. The second interpretation refers to Davidson's theory because, in case someone did something that caused the fire—in correspondence with the *accordion-effect*[68] –, we would describe the doing as an act of making a fire. But the ordinary use of the expression does not mean: *x* is the agent in the sense of Davidson's view, because with the expression we ascribe intentions. For him, this is not the case.

speech acts Davidson makes a distinction of three sorts of intentions: 1. "ulterior" intentions, that is, ends we achieve by non-linguistic means; 2. linguistic utterances which are produced with the intended forces, for example, assertions, commands, jokes, or questions and so on; and 3. strict semantic intentions, that is, the speaker or writer intends that his words will be interpreted with a certain meaning; Davidson, Locating Literary Language (1983), 170-71. In: Truth, Language, and History. London 2005.

66 Davidson, How is Weakness of the Will Possible (1970), 39. In: Action and Events.

67 Davidson, Intending (1978), 88. In: Actions and Events.

68 On Austin, Feinberg, see Geographical Overview, I 1. (a), in this book.

Intentions are no sufficient conditions of any ascription of action because g, the action x, for example, the spilling of the coffee, may be the case if non-p, for example, "James" does not have the intention of doing it.

It is certainly not absurd to explicate the expression "x brings about c" in Davidson's view. In this case, explication means finding a technical equivalence for a vernacular talk. If we interpreted the expression this way, we could ask the question to this account: how do we ascribe propositional attitudes with these expressions? The ascription of attitudes has to be handled on this basis: normally we use the expression "x brings about c", in respect of doing c, to ascribe intentions. If a speaker uttered in a given situation s "James did x with the intention to do a", we would interpret the expression in such a way that, by using his words, the speaker s refers to the same state that conventionally corresponds to "I want to (shall) do a". But "doing something willfully" is the case only if I do it intentionally. When interpreting the utterance "I want (shall) to do something, now", we interpret the word "want to" as an expression of an attitude. But we do not need any mysterious acts of will. If we make the assumption that the series of acts overlap (Anscombe)—though I think it is a misleading assumption—, the answer to the question of the identity of actions presupposes that all parts of actions refer to the performed action, and all that tells us about the same entity. The question:

1. Why does James give a piano concert?

must be distinguished from the question:

2. Why does James play the piano?

The questions (1) and (2) may refer to the same event, but (1) gives us nor answer to the question of the intention of playing the piano; the answer could be, for example, "James was invited to do it". Only then, provided that we know the intention, could we answer (2), for example, James plays the piano because he wants to show his artistic playing. Therefore intentions, also as mental items, play a role for explaining action. But we do not explain the real happening of events, but *why* a certain event happens or not.

Davidson had recognized in continuation the *problem of intention*; he wrote, "At one time (about twenty-five years ago, when I wrote "Actions, Reasons and Causes") I thought there were no such states as intending; here were just intentional actions. This was, I now believe, an error. This is clear in the case where an intention is formed long before the intended action is performed, and ever clearer in the case where the intended action is never performed. Intentions are also required to explain how complex actions are monitored and controlled." He continues, "We don't usually "form" intentions, we just come to have them."[69] But this is not a modification of his desire-belief explanation of actions in principle: an agent which is moved by an all-out judgment is moved by the causal force of the desire; he calls such a disposition *pro attitude*.[70] Therefore he has not given up his desire-belief explanation in general. The desire-belief theory is also not modified in principle when he writes, "Certainly it is true that if some event, say my arm going up, is an action, then there must also be an intention. But in my view, the intention is not part of the action, but a cause of it. Just as nothing is added to my telephoning my friend when that act becomes a thanking, so noting I added to my arm going up if that event is caused by an intention."[71] Intentions are dispositions because our strongest judgment as intention is moved by a desire. Desires are dispositions and dispositions are ultimately physical states. If not, the monism of the mental and physical, the shared ontology of both, would be given up. And this characterization is not falsified thereby that the *Davidson-view* does not go along with the Humean desire-belief explanation substantially because also beliefs and desires are causal condition of actions.[72] This leads us to the problem of the motivational strength of the causation of actions. Quine made a distinction between the *mental*, the *behavioral*, and the *physical*. Language is a disposition and dispositions are a physical trait. The mental is, for him, not a subject of a serious science, but the mental language is useful for everyday descriptions and explanations. On this level, the talk of the mental is not denied.[73]

---

69 Davidson, Problems in the Explanation of Action (1987), 106, 107, 105-08. In: Problems of Rationality.

70 Davidson, Could There be a Science of Rationality? (1995), 108. In: Problems of Rationality.

71 Davidson, Could There be a Science of Rationality?, 105. In: Problems of Rationality. The causal role of intentions and their causal self-referentiality is also emphasized by J. R. Searle, Intentionality. Cambridge 1983: 86. See also The Intentionality of the Intention and Action. Inquiry 22 1979, 253-80.

72 Davidson, Expression Evaluation (1984), 26. In: Problems of Rationality.

73 On Quine and his behaviorism Davidson, Could There be a Science of Rationality? (1995), 118-21. In: Problems of Rationality.

Intentions and *beliefs* are similar, not only in the mentioned issue at the beginning of the chapter—desirable actions are dependent on beliefs that something will be the case; if not, there cannot be a respective intention—but also in another point because they are not to analyze like the assent to the verifying of the truth-condition of thoughts only, but primarily as a practical consistency to act in conformity with practical thoughts and their fulfillment conditions. They are to express in the form: *I shall (want) to do a*. But the expression is a fragment. It does not stand alone and is not self-sufficient. It refers recursively to the question, "What shall I (we) do?" and, "Which course of action is the best to take for me, for us or for him?" in accordance with a deliberation. Deliberation is connected with two tasks, a theoretical and a practical. The theoretical task is to answer the question, "Which course of action is the best to take?" and the practical task is to act in conformity with the theoretical one. This is also the case if our strongest desires are of a different kind.[74] Here we recognize a problem in principle: why do we stop our deliberation to finish our theoretical task? This refers to the problem of the unification of thought, meaning and action and at the same time of theoretical and practical thinking because the end of our deliberation is a *decision* and we are trained to do this and to decide in certain situations. In a further step, intentions are to specify to practical thoughts: practical thoughts imply intentions. The analysis of the word *because* in action-explaining sentences requires a modified answer to the relation between an intention and an intentional action, so that we find a way to analyze intentions with a non-Davidsonian account. The logical relation is to re-interpret as a practical syllogism. But the re-interpretation of an explanatory redescription by practical syllogism does not show us that the action is desirable to do, and it is not a redescription of the actual reasoning of an agent.

---

74 See K. Baier, The Moral Point of View. A rational Basis of Ethics. New York 1958, 49.

(c) Practical Thought

> When an intention is formed we go from a stage in
> which we perceive, or imagine that we perceive, the
> attractions and drawbacks of a course of action to
> a stage in which we commit ourselves to act. This
> may be just another pro-attitude, but an intention,
> unlike other desires or pro-attitudes, is not merely
> conditional or prima facie.
>
> D. Davidson[75]

(i) Situation

S. Hampshire, for example, has emphasized that empiricist theories of perception of Berkeley, Hume and their successors have epistemically made a deep mistake because they make the assumption of a passive observer who has impressions from outside the mind as a basic model in epistemology.[76] He argues that the reference to something in my environment, the natural, pre-social gesture we perform with intentions, is the link on which the communication about physical things depends.[77] Davidson calls this the pre-linguistic situation of triangulation. Intentions are directed to situations: "Even the etymology of the word 'intention' suggests that the gesture of pointing from a place to a place is the natural and concrete expression of intention".[78] Therefore pre-social gestures performed with intentions link the communication about external things and events. But the inside-outside differentiation of organism, population, social system and their environment is the absolute distinction which entails consequences in the theory of perception, mind, and action. Every observer, thinker and interpreter does not stand out-

75 D. Davidson, Problems in the Explanation of Action (1987), 107, 105. In: Problems of Rationality.
76 In this model, the own body is also outside, Davidson, Problems in the Explanation of Action (1987), 46-7. In: Problems of Rationality.
77 Hampshire, Thought and Action, 90-168. From my point of view this type of communication can only work when the participants recognize regularities. It is hard to image how this level of communication switches to a type of communication which is differentiated by illocutionary and propositional components explicitly. With natural, pre-social gestures we cannot (re-) identify entities. This is only possible on the lingual level.
78 Davidson, Problems in the Explanation of Action (1987), 54-55. In: Problems of Rationality.

side the world. Thinking, stating and directive acts are cognitive activities of creatures that can identify things, events, others and themselves to which they refer. But to identify the reference-relation and complete it with predicative expression requires having a language within which we express reference and predication. The inside-outside differentiation entails that by communication we do not reach the consciousnesses of other minds. There are no ideal situations of exchange between minds, their thoughts, feelings, and emotions; therefore all understanding of others is fragmentary in nature and gradual. But communication works without such connections because *on the level of lingual communication meaning is autonomous*. We can communicate without language, but on the lingual level we can only ascribe attitudes. We can only know whether a sentence has fulfillment conditions like truth and compliance conditions or whether the sentence has a meaning, if we are successful in ascribing propositional attitudes and if we describe actions as connected with intentions. This is not disputed. But this leads us also to the question whereby the agent is committed by himself.

In order to give an answer to the question of the relationship between intention and intentional actions, it is necessary in the first step to determine our speaking about a *situation of acting*. An agent does not introspectively perceive that and how belief, desire and intention and other attitudes work together. This leads us to the problem of the conceptual and causal relation of explaining actions. An intention emerges in stages, that is, an intention to doing something, if the agent has a belief, a want, preferences and particular abilities that are brought together: the agent expects that the course of doing (action) fulfills his want, preference are met by particular events in the future as he intends. Therefore belief and desire must play together. Traditionally this was called *practical reasoning*. The intention is formed if in a given situation the agent perceives or imagines that he commits himself to a particular doing. This is not only another pro attitude, but an *intention*. I call this a *practical commitment*. Such commitments give the unconditional judgment its motivational strength. But it may be also the case that our virtue is too week and that we are dominated by inner or outer constraints in our doings. They may be successful or not.

The following characterization is helpful to understand the situation of acting:

* If any agent intends to do the action *a* in the situation *b* and forms his relevant beliefs, we suppose that:

1. the agent has the belief that he is—under certain descriptions and recognitions—in the situation *b*, and in so far he has no contradicting intentions, so
2. he will do *a* and do intentionally *a*,
3. it is to suppose: he has the ability to do *a* in *b*,
4. he is not prevented and is really in *b*,
5. he does not do *a*, if he does not *try* to do *a*: actions are a result of *trying*,
6. his actions could be successful or not.

The conceptualized resources of situations from the agent's and interpreter's (observer's) point of view is that they image the distinction between trying (doing) and what is done as redescribed and re-interpretated as an action. One must distinguish between *intending* but not *succeeding* as the opposite of *attempt* and *success*. Furthermore one must distinguish between an attempt which was *not successful* and an attempt which reached its goal *successfully* for each class of action and their ascription. This is to assume for the interpreter but also from an agent's point of view. Also an agent himself must be able to distinguish between what his intent is and what he achieves or not. The distinction of what counts as *trying* and *intending* to reach a goal by his belief takes effect in the conceptual resources of a theory of agent. This is the reason why in epistemic considerations we take in the first person authority, that is, the thinker (speaker, agent) and the object of thought, which is not explained away by an *explanatory view* of such authority. For Davidson, for example, first person authority does not have an epistemic basis, for Peter and Peter* on the Twin Earth do not have the same phenomenological states caused by different types of entity. They cannot perform different types of action; but, for example, going to opera meeting friends or want to be alone in the crowd, Peter and Peter* perform not only a particular action in the twins but also *types of action*. The types are abstracted from the situation of doing. Therefore the individuation conditions of their attitudes are not the same. The distinction between what counts as trying and intending to reach a goal by Peter's belief is the epistemic basis of first person authority, that is, between the particular relation of the thinker (speaker, agent) and the content of thoughts. It is not a priori excluded that there are not different reference relations; we individuate the mental states and the reference of explanatory redescription.

But do we have a particular knowledge of our own actions?

For Anscombe, the assumption of such knowledge of our own action is a fault. She calls such knowledge: *knowledge without observation*.[79] But to characterize the first person authority by such knowledge leads to some misunderstandings. If someone makes an occasion happen by raising his arm, then he normally know "that he raises his arm". But he cannot conclude his knowledge that ... from a distinguished peace of his certainty like the certainty that he raises his arm. The only certainty the agent has is that he has tried to raise his arm. In such cases, an agent has a knowledge without observation because his trying must be distinguished—also as an item of behavior—from what we report by our observation of another's acting. The knowledge that someone does something, his first person authority, is to distinguish from the knowledge that the result of his trying has a certain effect. The latter is an empirical knowledge. *Trying* something is an evidence for an interpreter (observer) that a doing is a mental one. This doing has a meaning (trying) that we can describe with the phrase, "What was relevant to do?" This was also emphasized by Strawson, Searle, D. Hodcroft, J. Hornsby, Aune, Hampshire, B. O'Shauglnessy, and others.[80] For Davidson, trying is of no importance because "... it may seem a difficulty that primitive actions do not accommodate the concept of trying, for primitive actions are ones we just do—nothing can stand in the way, so to speak. But surely, the critic will say, there are some things we must strive to do (like hit the bull's eye). Once more the same sort of answer serves. Trying to do one thing may be simply doing another. I try to turn on the light by flicking the switch, but I simply flick the switch. Or perhaps even that is, on occasion, an attempt. Still, the attempt consists of something I can do without trying; just move my hand, perhaps."[81] His argument results from the point of view of exemplifying—and also ascribing—actions directly to an agent. If someone makes an occasion happen by raising his arm, then he normally knows "that he raises his arm". But he cannot conclude his knowing that ... from a separate piece of certainty, for example, his certainty that he raises his arm. The only certainty he

79 Anscombe, Intention, 13-15.
80 In particular B. O'Shaughnessy, Trying (As the Mental, Pineal Gland), 52, 65. In: Mele (ed.), Philosophy of Action, Oxford 1997. He insists that intentional agent must *try* in order to act intentionally. From his point of view trying is an independent mental event which causes a body movement and occurs simultaneously.
81 Davidson, Agency (1971), 60. In: Action and Events. Oxford 1980.

can dispose about is that he has tried to raise his arm. *The description of trying is a mental one, but not one of a body movement only.* In this situation, people have a knowledge without observation (Anscombe) because the *attempt*—also as item of behavior—is to separate from the report of his doing by observation. This is the answer to the question why the knowledge that someone does something is to distinguish from the knowledge that a result of trying has a certain effect.

Situations of acting are features of a more or less changeable *basic situation* and consist of physical, biological, social, and cultural entities, events and their properties. In this context we could also speak of classes of situations. The elementary framework of the systematizing of conceptual recourses consists of

1. the actor system (organic -, personal -, social -, cultural system),
2. the situation of acting and their entities and
3. the environments.

This framework is to characterize in such a way that it is not empty with respect to the supposed universe. Thereby the universe is causally significant for the interpretation of the framework. If there is a variation of the components of the domain of values of the fulfillment conditions of the framework, then this is consequential for the domain of values of the ordering of the components: if the truth conditions are false, then something is wrong with the entities we have assumed; when Peter comes on Monday to go fishing, he will make the existence presupposition that there are fishes in the river; when there are no fishes there he will suppose that the universe is empty.

If we talk of the *context of situations*, the word "context" refers to theoretical and cognitive abstractions. The *definition of situation* assumes for its description an *identity of contexts*. If the context changes, there is the same statement or description, but the speaker reference and the reference of singular terms like names, definite descriptions, or indexicals are not the same; therefore, the speaker performs another illocutionary act, for example, "Yesterday, the stairs on the third floor were burning", as a statement about an event in difference to the same sentence as an accusation in legal proceedings. But we can only identify situations basically if there is an interdependency of the objective localization and the demonstrative identification of entities of awareness. Demonstrative singular terms like "here", "this", "now", "that" are semantic classes. They are to connect with other expressions by the identity sign, that is, we use them in a way that they are to substitute in different situations. The use in different situations of demonstratives is dependent on the objective localization.[82]

The causal significance of the universe of the interpretation of the framework is the subject of the re-interpretation of situation of acting epistemically; that means asking what constitutes the relationship between language and world, agent (groups, social systems) and environment. The problem is:

What gives perceptions, attitudes, signs, sentences, whatever, their content?

This leads us back to the new problems in philosophy of mind since the eighties, the thought-experiments of Putnam and Burge on the individuation of mental states. What mental states are is to answer by their *condition of individuation*. The question is:

How are mental states to individuate by the behavior of an agent and its ordinary interaction with the environment?

The common-sense explanation involves propositional attitudes. Therefore the question, "How is their content to individuate?" must be answered. I do not argue that there is a simple relation between the extern stimulus and the resulting thought because conceptual resources and theoretical knowledge are not to explain by such a mechanism. This is a problem in epistemology, philosophy of language, and also in cognitive science and cognitive psychological explanations. Parts of modern epistemology which assume that we are aware of the unconceptualized given go wrong. The turn against classical empiricism is made, for example, by Austin, Sellars, Davidson, and others.[83]

From an epistemical perspective, the problem is:

How do perceptions (perceptional sentences) get their content?

Such sentences do not get their content from sense data, but their empirical content is caused in situations in which we accept and reject them, that is, in situations where we learn about fulfillment conditions of such sentences.[84] If we argue that beliefs, desires and intentions are partially caused by the history of their causation and we individuate action on the same level like propositional attitudes, then we have to give an answer to the question *whether there is something like a subjective (narrow) content of attitudes.* This is obvious because we are interested

82 See E. Tugendhat, Vorlesungen zur Einführung in die sprachanalytische Philosophie. Frankfurt am Main 1976, 426-39.

83 On critique on this tradition J. Fodor, LOT II The Language of Thought Revisited. Oxford 2008.

84 Davidson, Seeing Through Language (1997), on perceptional sentences, 137-8. In: Truth, Language, and History. Oxford 2005.

in the description, prediction, and explanation of intentional actions and at the same time in pairing attitudes to the agents. It has been discussed since the eighties that the leading problem of Fodor's theory is: how do we solve the difficulty of bringing together the internalistic computer theory and an externalization of mental content? Stich, for example, has argued that the two cannot be harmonized: a representational theory of mind whose generalizations of cognitive psychology refer to content, and the same time a computational theory of mind which does not refer to content.[85] The question is:

* Does *local causality* imply local individuation or individualistic supervenience?[86]

Most philosophers would agree about the following:

1. Distal events cause *local events* by a chain of mediated causes, and
2. local behavior of an organism is determinated by the *inner neural structure* which determine the local causes that take effect in the inner neural structure.
3. But this is not an argument in favor of the assumption that the *mental states*
are to individuate and to locate by the *local causes* and *effects*.

Causality is local, but the principles of individuation reflect causes by the particular physical environment within which the organism is embedded. Many generalizations in psychology refer to causal relations between mental states and processes and their distal causes and effects. The question is in general:

* Cognitive psychological explanations refer to mental *different* states or *types of mental* if the neural structure is identical and explain thereby behavioral regularities also in the cases where the distal causes are different. In other cases it may be or is a successful explanatory strategy to pair mental states to the same type, also in case they are different in their neural structure if the distal causation is different.

85 S. Stich, Narrow Content meets Fat Syntax, 239-54. In: B. Loewer, G. Rey (eds.). Meaning and Mind. Fodor and his Critics. Cambridge Mass. 1991.
86 On the versions of supervenience Rogler, Preyer, Materialismus, anomaler Monismus und mentale Kausalität. Zur gegenwärtigen Philosophie des Mentalen bei Donald Davidson und David Lewis, 43-50.

Fodor's critique on Burge is that *local causality requires also local individuation and the causal power is not to divide*. Fodor does not accept that the causal forces which are relevant for psychological explanations, are not to define by proximal or local causal relations. But distal causal relations are contextually variable. The identity of causal power cannot be relativized to different contexts. The problem is whether Fodor's metaphysical concept of causality for an individualistic understanding of psychology and of narrow content is really convincing.

But Fodor may be right in that the behavior of Peter and Peter* is comparable (similar), and we can explain it by the same psychological generalizations. By way of contrast, Burge/Putnam's thought-experiment ascribes (instances) distinct types of mental states (attitudes) because the individuation condition is externally to specify. In Burge's counterfactual situation the thinker's (speaker's, agent's) physical states are identical, described in an non-intentional language. But the social environment is not the same. Therefore *we ascribe no belief about arthritis to the thinker (speaker, agent) in the counterfactual situation.* In both cases the physical state are fixed, but the mental states differ. The thought-experiment is instructive because it shows that *the type of agent and situation* (definition of situation) *takes in the ascription of attitudes.*[87]

Peter and Peter* do not do the same thing if they drink something. They both perform not only a particular action, but also a *type* of action. Such types are abstracted from the situation of doing. On this level of abstraction we need narrow contents (intentional content) for the explanation of actions. This is also the problem of Davidson's anti-representationalism because it is not answered how we can pair intentional content to the abstract structure of the Unified Theory. For Davidson, attitudes are simply states and have no objects in a psychological and epistemic sense. The objects are the interpreter's own sentences for the ascription of attitudes. The problem is that the object language of the speaker may be richer or poorer than the language the interpreter uses

87 H. Putnam, The Meaning of 'Meaning' (1975), 215-71. In: Mind Language and Reality. Philosophical Papers (2 Vol.) Vol. 2. Cambridge 1975, T. Burge, Individualism and the Mental (1979), 100-50, Postcript to Individualism and the Mental 206, 151-181, Two Thought Experiments Reviewed (1982). In: Foundation of Mind. Oxford 2007, See also Fodor, Replies: 280-85. In: B. Loewer and G. Rey (eds.), Meaning and Mind. Fodor and his Critics, R. Schantz, *Wahrheit, Referenz und Realismus.* Eine Studie zur Sprachphilosophie und Metaphysik. Berlin 1996, 376-405.

for the ascription of attitudes. Holism, externalism and the basic rationality (charity) cannot bridge that.

The intelligible explanation of action is dependent on a type of propositional attitude, some narrow act types, and the object they involve. The distinction of narrow act-types in the Twins is not dependent on the token of a particular behavior. This is not in conflict with externalism in general because Burge's "instances of an objective kind" are types of objects, properties etc. which are in the environment of the agent, and no instances outside the Twins gives the perception its content. At the same time, *the epistemic differentiation (authorities) must take in the ascription of attitudes, and we do not individuate attitudinal content by an external causal relation we perceive in our environment.* The relevance of the epistemic differentiation takes effect in the *re-interpretation of the intentional expression* because every interpreter (translator, ethnologist, social scientist, ordinary speaker) assumes some of his everyday life knowledge, semantics, and science to homogenize translation (interpretation) from his point of view. The success of interpretation is the criterion for deciding whether all these work.

(ii) Intention

> Certainly it is true that if some event, say my arm going up, is an action, then there must also be an intention.
>
> D. Davidson[88]

The central problem in the philosophy of action is:

What are actions? How are intentional actions to be explained *as* intentional ones?

It is not disputed that every successful ascription of propositional attitudes and description actions is connected with intentions. Intentional actions are purposive behavior and in some cases, as Aristotle argued, the purpose is the doing of the action itself. It is widely accepted that an intentional action is done for a reason (desires and beliefs). But intentions link reasons and action. The distinction between intentional and non-intentional actions is itself not disputed.

What is the problem of intention? Some philosophers have argued that intention does not play a significant role in the theory of inten-

---

88 D. Davidson, Problems in the Explanation of Action (1987), 105. In: Problems of Rationality.

tionality.[89] If we make the assumption that intentions are propositional attitudes then we must ask, and answer:

What role does the content of attitudes play when explaining action? What is the relation between intention and intentional action? What individuates the content of attitudes? Are intentions real mental items or not?

Davidson's identity-theses and his syncategorematical account of intention argue the *criterion of agency* is semantically *intensional* and *the expression of agency* is *extensional*. There are *classes of events* that are actions. The price paid by this account is that intentions are no mental items and are no intentional entities as such. But there is no intention without an intentional content. Intentions are propositional attitudes, and their connections with the expression of practical thought show us how the *intent* makes something happen (self-reference), that is, a future event that does *not* exist and the future event outside the thinker (speaker, agent) which motivates the intentional content itself is to grasp.

How do we express practical thoughts, and how are practical thoughts connected with intention?

I will call "*x* shall do *a*" an *expression of an intention*. Such sentences seem to be like statements, but they are no predictions.[90] These sentences express an intention as a result of a decision born by a want. A *practical question* like, "What shall I do?" has an *intention sentence* as its complement. If we make the assumption that intentions are partially born by *wants*—I intend what I want and decide—, we could say that only the mastering of situations of actions causes the building of an intention in a certain way. This explains also the motivational strength and the practical consistency of an agent because the virtue of our capacity moves us to do something or not. Intending to do something is directed by the motivation of the agent to bring about particular issues. This explains also the *coordinative* function of intentions and why many philosophers make a distinction between proximal and distal intentions. A *proximal intention* is "an agent who intends A (beginning) at once—an agent who, as I shall say, proximally intends to A will A intentionally (beginning) straightaway, unless something prevents his

89 For example, J. R. Searle, Geist, Gehirn und Wissenschaft (1984). Frankfurt am Main 1986, 59.

90 Tugendhat, Vorlesungen zur Einführung in die sprachanalytische Philosophie, 110, is right when he argues, if one gives a promise and does not keep it, then we do not say "he made a mistake" but "he has not kept what he promised".

doing so or thwarts his efforts".[91] *Distal intentions* are components of a larger plan. They control behavior. But this involves also revisions and control of the goal orientation.[92] The Mele-problem is we have in particular to explain how the *motivational strength* of effective reasons works. I agree with him (and M. Brand) that beliefs themselves are not the representational content of intentions. But the origin of intentions does not entail that

1. an intention or a thought to do something have in themselves no particular effect on the manifest behavior of an agent, and
2. the connection of intentions and beliefs that we ascribe causes an intentional action in a given situation. How something is caused by our attitudes cannot be researched in detail by any interpreter.[93]

Intentions are directed to goals and future actions that the agent will perform from his beliefs and wants, desires, principles, whatever. For the analysis of intentions it is helpful to make the following distinctions:

1. Intentions $I_{(0)}$ as *constitutive intentions* of actions: this is an intentional acting (action) *e*, for example, an *intentional doing* to shoot a torpedo (Searle: intention-in-action[94]). $I_{(0)}$ is to distinguish from
2. the *prior intention* $I_{(p)}$ that is before it $I_{(0)}$, for example, the intention to sink the Bismarck, that is not constitutive for my action, for example, the same action could be done independently of a certain $I_{(p)}$ as, for example, the cannoneer can have the intention of shooting the torpedo to warn another ship. In general that means that $I_{(0)}$ are conditions of satisfaction of $I_{(p)}$.

But it may be that $I_{(0)}$ is not done with $I_{(p)}$, for example, the cannoneer intentionally torpedoes the ship, but not intentionally the Tirpitz. Davidson argues that the different effects and consequences are no parts

---

91 Mele, Springs of Action, 72
92 Mele, Springs of Action. On proximal intention, 137, on distal intentions, on acquisition and proximal intention, 180-81, on fundamental motivation of proximal intentions, wants and intensions, also independently of all-things-considered value judgments, 187-91, on proximal intentions and volition, 193, on modifications: 192, on the representational content of intentions: 110.
93 See the *climber-example*: Davidson, Freedom to Act (1973), 79. In: Actions and Events.
94 Searle, Rationality in Action, Cambridge 2001, 44.

of actions, but there is only one deed we redescribe in different ways, for example, as unintended consequences or unintended characteristics. Therefore it is, for him, no class of intentional action. If we assumed this we would say that the same action is at the same time intentional and non-intentional.[95]

3. A *motivated* intention $I_{(m)}$, for example, the motivation to certain actions A with it we try to strive to fulfill an intention $I_{(p)}$.

4. $I_{(m)}$ could be *reasons for actions* and its $I_{(i)}$. It is to make the assumption that $I_{(m)}$ in respect to an action A in many cases is an $I_{(i)}$ in reference to an other action A', for example, the action that the Bismarck sinks A as a contribution to win the sea battle A'. In such cases is A' not a result but a consequence A. A' supposes as condition of satisfaction the *cooperation* of agent for the goal-attainment of $I_{(p)}$.[96]

But $I_{(m)}$ is not strong enough to make the action desirable from the agent's point of view. A further condition is to satisfy, that is,

5. an *all-out judgment* "This action is desirable" $J_{(u)}$ forming the intention $I_{(i)}$ and I commit myself to do something. Acting is induced to cope with functional imperatives of situations that cause our actions under certain conditions that the agent has recognized (and knows). This is also implied in the all-out judgments that form intentions. The unconditional imperative of such judgments are caused by functional imperatives of the coping of situations of acting, for example, torpedo the Bismarck A as a contribution of the cooperation to win the sea battle A' as a contribution to end the Second World War A". But the judgment itself is not the intention.

6. *Intentions are self-referential*, but they have a content.

What is the *content of intention*?

There are particular problems to determine such content like in the case of other conative attitudes because their content does not stand alone as in the case of beliefs.

Many philosophers could agree that we solve the problem of conative attitude when we determine the content of intentions with their fulfillment conditions and add that they have be to execute, that is, an agent or a group fulfills an intention to do x if and only if the agent

---

95 Davidson, Agency (1971), 46-47, Freedom to Act (1973): 71. In: Actions and Events. On the problem of the right causation with regart to the anomalous *external* and *lunatic internal* (climber-example) causal chains, 78-79.

96 On the three distinctions J. Nida-Rümelin, Kritik des Konsequentialismus. München 1993, 31-35.

or the group executes x and does it intentionally.[97] But intentions are *self-referential*; therefore *the contents as their fulfillment conditions are to execute as individuation conditions*. This condition is not to describe by neurological and physical states as a local microstructure. The individuation of mental state and intention are no subject of physical science. The explanation of action assumes propositional attitudes on the thinker's (speaker's, agent's) side that we individuate by their "that-clause". The thinker's (speaker's, agent's) belief that Darmstadt in Germany is in the South of Frankfurt am Main and Heidelberg is in the South of Darmstadt are different beliefs (that-clauses), thereby we characterize the attitudes he has. We individuate such clauses externally. But the problem is that that-clauses are too fine-grained to individuate mental contents.[98]

But does the distal cause dominate the proximal cause?

Externalism conflicts with the thinker's (speaker's) intuition about the identity of his own mental states. This leads us to the problem of practical thought. We have to distinguish between fulfillment conditions, success and intrinsic values of actions.

7. *Cooperations* are based on *structural intentions* as the basic unit of collective intentions of members of groups. Nida-Rümelin analyzes intentions as features of a *structural rationality* (a structural intention), that is, if I have the intention to perform a particular action and I have a descriptive belief that the doing of h requires the actions $h_1, \ldots h_n$, I built such intention.[99] People often share thoughts and also feelings. In the case of a social belief the relevant belief connects an agent with other beliefs they share. Therefore we call them *we-attitudes* and *intentions*. Such we-attitudes of different sorts are the instances of so-called collective intentionality. We ascribe such shared attitudes to the components of the social universe.[100]

Let us make three distinctions about collective attitudes (intentionality):

---

97 For example, Mele, Springs of Action, 208.

98 See B. Loar, Social Contents and Psychological Contents, 99-110. In: R.H. Grimm, D.D. Merrill (eds.), Contents of Thoughts. Tucson 1988.

99 J. Nida-Rümelin, Strukturelle Rationalität. Ein philosophischer Essay über praktische Vernunft. Stuttgart 2001, 121, 65. See on Nida-Rümelin, Structural Intention http://www.protosociology.de/on-philosophy.html

100 The social is not completely to characterize by collective intentionality. The characteristic of the social universe is to take in, and also vocabulary of membership and the authority system.

1. A collective goal (collectivity orientation) is the propositional content of a we-want (we-goal).
2. This goal is intended by some agent.
3. There is a collective goal.[101]

Tuomela makes the distinction between a *weak* and a *full-blown* collective intention. The weaker version is that some people have a shared *we*-goal, that is, they know that they have it. This is a *reflexive condition*: *x* knows that *y* knows that *x* knows that *p*. The reflexive condition of knowing is a necessary condition of their plans.

The stronger, *full-blown intention* is the intended notion itself. This implies the *participants'* intentions of the agents but not in all cases the based-planed intention. This involves the shared goal-orientated doings to reach the end of the goal, shared goal-orientated doings, and also a collective control. The latter implies that the alternatives of the agents are restricted by their preferences. Therefore, these *restrictions* are based on the intention and the commitment of the participants. *Aim intentions* and *aim goals* (action intentions) are different from *intention-in-action* (intentional action). The agent can satisfy and is committed to the content to the collective intention. Tuomela argues that these connections between the beliefs of the agents and, at the same time, the satisfaction of the acceptance of a collective goal among participants is of non-contingent *quasi-conceptual grounds*. *Full-blown intentions* are the strongest sort of collective intentions. The basic concept of Tuomela's analysis is the we-attitude of *acting together to reach a collective goal*.

Nida-Rümelin and Tuomela give a fruitful analysis and framework for the analysis of *structural (collective) intentions.*[102] From my point of

101 There is no significant difference in substance between the analysis of Nida-Rümelin and Tuomela. Tuomela, The Philosophy of Sociality. A Collective Acceptance View. Cambridge GB 2002, 19, on a detailed analysis, see also: 17-39, on a stylized summary of *intention act together*, 27. On the debate on collective beliefs and social ontology, see also ProtoSociology Vol. 18-19 2003: Understanding the Social II: Philosophy of Sociality. Edited by R. Tuomela, G. Preyer, G. Peter, Vol. 16 2002: Understanding the Social I: New Perspectives from Epistemology, M. Gilbert, Sociality and Responsibility. New Essays in Plural Subject Theory. Lanham 2000, P. Pettit, A Theory of Freedom. From the Psychology to the Politics of Agency. Cambridge 2001.
102 See also my reviews, Ein Meister aus dem Norden. R. Tuomela, Philosophy of Social Practices. The Collective Acceptance View. Cambridge

view, one must continue to the membership condition of social systems which is not in conflict with the substance of their framework. The reason to do this is that the ascription of attitudes works together with the *social frame of reference*. Within this frame, the members of the social system assume that the ascription of attitudes must correlate with the social roles and status of members that they fulfill by certain conditions of their doings. This is significant for structural intentions because, if the restrictions of the social frame are given, the commitment bonds the particular agent. Therefore I have introduced such restrictions with reference to single agents or members of groups as *practical commitment*. Such commitments are born by $I_{(m)}$ and $J_{(u)}$ and the *condition of membership*. This implies that more than one agent satisfies the intended propositional content of the goal; it is also to apply to the particular collectivity and at the same time to the collective agent. Tuomela calls that the *collectivity-condition*. The contents of intention and of we-want are not to analyze differently in substance.[103] The content of both is to execute, and this is the role of such content in both cases.

We see that there is a connection between *intentions* and *practical thoughts* and the *orientation of their execution*. In the case of *collective intentionality* the execution is organized among the members of social systems, for example, a social group. Another point is that intentions are in common with decisions because in deciding to x intentions are formed to do it.[104] The principal difference between desires and intentions is that I may have many desires without solving any practical questions. Intention requires also practical thought.

I will comment on *commitments* in the framework of structural intentions from a sociological point of view, which I have analyzed in another context.[105] Commitments are restrictions that form a social structure by borderlines of membership in social systems. Every communication which is an event has a selective effect that reduces pos-

2002. In: Philosophische Rundschau 4 2003, R. Tuomela, Cooperations. Philosophical Series 82. Dordrecht 2000. In: Philosophischer Literaturanzeiger 1 2004; J. Nida-Rümelin, Über menschliche Freiheit. Stuttgart 2005. In: Zeitschrift für Philosophische Forschung 1 2006.

103 Tuomela, The Philosophy of Social Practices. A Collective Acceptance View, 29-30.

104 But this is not to generalize, see Mele, Springs of Action, 141. On intentions and desires, 166-170.

105 Preyer, Soziologische Theorie der Gegenwartsgesellschaft. Mitgliedschaftstheoretische Untersuchungen: on the function of commitments, 117-20.

sibilities and reveals something. Therefore commitments are a medium that selects the chances of continuation of communication. It is not an essential feature that commitments are reasonable, but their function is to stabilize expectation. A reasonable evaluation can be handed in later and we explain this by selectively formed commitments that are not disputed. It is often the case that from our free choice we conclude the strength of a commitment we have, for example, I have signed a working contract and I am bound to go conform with the commitment and the corporate culture in the company where I work now. Therefore commitments can also couple members with dissent and in spite of intended differences among them. The communicative medium of commitment can be coupled, to a stronger or a weaker degree, to the conditions of membership, for example, in ethnic groups, or in the kinship system; in some subculture group they are coupled in a stronger way than in formal organizations. In the same way the commitments are not at all to identify with acceptance or consent. Commitments are media of membership.

(iii) Practical Thought

Actions have causal consequences, but they are not only results of our conative attitudes and our descriptive beliefs.[106] They are also a result of *deliberations*. We have also to take into play that some doings have an *intrinsic value*. It is not disputed that there are some basic beliefs and conative attitudes of members of social systems we do not dispose about because for their members they are self-evident. *Practical thought* implies *intentions* built from their *definition of situations*.

How do we describe such practical thoughts?

Such thought implies *intentions* built from their *definition of situations*. The description has to emphasize its feature of interpersonal verification. We describe such thoughts in the way:

* People are *able* to do *a*, for example, *moving* the hand, if *b*, for example, opening the window, is *necessary* for tentatively everyone to *reach the goal c*, for example, warming up the room and so a *situation* happens which is pleasant for the guests and ... Such thoughts imply a generalization and a successful confirmation.[107]

---

106 Nida-Rümelin, Strukturelle Rationalität, 123.
107 On the role of these generalizations, see II 2., in this book.

If this is the case, then we presuppose for the ascription of actions a connection between *beliefs* (reasons), the conformity with the *agent-practical consistency* and given *actions*. Practical thoughts would be our *strongest beliefs* that we express in *unconditional judgments* as our *goal orientations*. It is fruitful to distinguish two points for the analysis of the relationship between *beliefs* and *intentions*:

1. *Thought* is to distinguish from *belief* and *intention*. With belief, not with thought, we claim their holding-true. "Having a thought requires that there be a background of beliefs, but having a particular thought does not depend on the state of belief with respect to that very thought. . . . I have the thought of going to the concert, but until I decide whether to go, I have no fixed belief that I will go; until that time, I merely entertain the thought. . . . a thought is defined by a system of beliefs, but is itself autonomous with respect to belief."[108] Thought has a quasi-logical structure, so we can deduct an inference from them.

2. *Practical thought* supposes that the conditions of his applications are satisfied. We express such thoughts in *intention sentences*. In so far we could make the following assumptions:

1. from the *thought a*, for example, that if x, then y

is to conclude

2. the *practical thinking b* in the form: "I intend to do x now ".

Practical thought is dependent on *true belief* and *intentions*, which can be fulfilled:

3. the *truth of the belief* that c, that is, the situation x or a certain action exists that brings about the intended result.

The *thought a* is to distinguish from the *belief* that c and also from the *intentions* $I_{(p,o,m)}$ and $I_{(u)}$.

The distinction between *thought, belief, intention, all-out judgment* and the *action* is dependent on the condition that the agent and the interpreter have some fulfilled attitudes caused by their situation of do-

---

108 Davidson, Thought and Talk (1975), 157. In: Inquiries into Truth and Interpretation. Oxford 1984.

ing, and they have a self-consciousness about the attitudes they image or vision. That is, from the agent's point of view there is a *projection of expectations* and *expectations of expectations ...* to a future time-point. This goes along with the definition and the recognition of a situation with which both are confronted and which they describe as the same activity (doing) as before, namely the same that they perceive externally without intending something. This is not an interpretation of an *omniscient observer's (interpreter's)* point of view, but a reflection to their *conceptual resources* to make a distinction, no matter whether linguistic or not. It is a necessary truth that the agent and interpreter can decide gradually about knowledge and what is to be done in a certain situation. How thoughts are to introduce in a practical inference is a question of the logic of practical reasoning.

(d) An Intentional Explanation

Davidson has modified his first causal analysis of the word *because* and takes in the explanation of action the distinction of the relations between actions and desire-belief pairs: firstly, a logical relation between the content of the attitudes and the desirability about the action, and secondly the causal role of primary reasons.[109] Both conditions are necessary, but not sufficient. Therefore we interpret the word *because* in action explained sentences not only *causal*, but also *logical*. But in the continuous response on his first version of primary reasons he has argued that the relationship between reasons— propositional attitudes in general — and actions is to specify as an intention as a cause, not as a part of the action. His concept of intention is that we do not usually form intentions, we have them.[110] Raz, for example, makes a distinction between *guiding reasons* as facts; for example, something which motivates us including true beliefs, moral principles, desires, and explanatory reasons, that is, the mental states of people whose doings we will explain.[111] *Explanatory reasons* suppose guiding reasons. Therefore explanatory reasons are to explain by guiding reason. But the

---

109 Davidson, Paradoxes of Irrationality (1982), 173. In: Problems of Rationality.

110 Davidson, Problems in the Explanation of Action (1987), 106-07, 107. In: Problems of Rationality.

111 J. Raz, Introduction, 4. In: Raz (ed.), *Practical Reasoning*, Oxford 1978.

reverse is not the case. We distinguish acting *with* a reason from acting *for* it. For the latter, beliefs and desires have a causal power, if any. It is the reason *for which* the agent performs that action. That is the action that the agent intends and the goal that he achieves or not. But this is the intentional content that the agent intends. There is a logical (conceptual) connection between both, which takes effect in our resources of explanatory redescription as a attribution and the application of the act-constitutive principles. If the action is rationalized, we redescribe it as intentional so that the agent has a pro or con attitude toward the action. The interpreter takes into play that the agent has an attitude toward the properties of the action as intentional content. This explains us the role of *intention*: what stops a reason (reasoning, deliberation) is the intention built by a *decision*. Therefore practical thought implies an intention. Desires may explain events which happen but not actions *done* by an agent. The role of intention explains us also freedom. But I do not argue that all intentional actions are free.

I have argued that *practical thought implies intention* that we specify by stating the conditions of doing. The meaning of *because* in sentences that explain action takes reference to these conditions as reasons why something is done, that is, we explain actions with the ascription of beliefs, desires and also complex intentions. This is the characteristic of teleological explanation but not of explanation in general.[112] Explanations of action are not causal because reasons for action are not logically independent of their causes and the content of attitudes of the agent is to take in the explanation, and this content explains the action rather than the causes of it. But this does not exclude that mental states are partially to individuate externally. On the other hand first person authority as an epistemic factor is not rejected by externalism. Evidential considerations are authoritative with respect to the content of our intentional states. Therefore externalism does not reject these factors. I have called this the *epistemic restrictions of interpretation* in general. In difference to perceptions, intentional-states are an instance of self-ascription and ascriptions from the third person point of view employ that-clauses. There is no disagreement among philosophers, externalists and internalists that an agent (speaker) *knows what he thinks*, and just this is a condition of communication. At the same time such states are self-referential, as the agent knows. Therefore I accept the *epistemic*

---

112 On the difference between reasons explanations and explanations of physics, Davidson, Problems in the Explanation of Action (1987), 109-116. In: Problems of Rationality.

basis of first person authority in respect of certain states. He displays the individuation condition to the agent at the moment he speaks/talks/ thinks about, and for all other states the epistemic authority is not given, that is, there is no relation between the thinker/speaker and the object of thoughts. The epistemic first person authority is a knowledge without observation or empirical investigations we have. This is a way to reinterpret the egocentric-public distinction. Intentional behavior is to explain by propositional attitudes. Their ascription presupposes the explanatory significance of their content within the *ontological frame-work* the agent (speaker) and interpreter share. Therefore it may be *counterfactual frameworks* of the ascription of attitudes. On the other hand we explain some body movement, for example, the movement of my hand turning on the light by empirical regularities which are not being intentional. But the physical cause of behavior is not to pick out by intentional descriptions.

Tentatively I will give the following *intentional explanation* of action.

* "James" did x $(I_{(0)})$ *because*

(1) he *intends a* to bring about the event E (= A') in the world W $(I_{(p)})$. The event E (= A' as result of A = act) is a causal consequence of the act x $(I_{(0)})$, that is the intentional doing.
(2) He has the *belief b* that he can bring about E (= A'), if he does x $(I_{(0)})$ in correspondence that it *is true* that the assumed situation exists.
(3) (i) $I_{(m)}$ strives to do $(I_{(0)})$,
  (ii) $(I_{(p)})$ is reasoned by $J_{(u)}$ and
  (iii) $I_{(m)}$ may be a reason for $(I_{(p)})$.
(4) His *intention a* $(I_{(i)})$ and his belief b imply the *practical premise c*:

* I *will/want/intend to bring about the event* E (= A') $(I_{(p)})$ and I can bring about (shall) this event E (A') expressed in $J_{(u)}$.

The formulation of the *practical premise* in accordance with our *practical thinking c*:

* I will/want/intend to do x $J_{(u)}$ is to interpret as a *expression of an intention* $(I_{(p)})$.

(5) "James" will act *in conformity with his practical consistency d* standing for the practical premise *c*, that is, expressed in a valid thinking *f* in a way:

* I *will/want/intend* to do *x* $(I_{(p)})$, if *x* $(I_{(0)}, A)$, then *E* (*A'*) and this is desirable $J_{(u)}$.

The *thought f* is distinct from the *belief b* and the *intention a* $(I_{(p)})$. *f* implies as a tacit *conclusion:*

(6) "James" conformity with his *practical consistency d* is to act in correspondence with his tacit conclusion *f* (I will/want/intent to do *x* $(I_{(0)})$.
(7) His conformity with his practical consistency *d* is expressed in the *practical thinking f*: I will/intent to do *x* $(I_{(0)})$, if *x* $(I_{(0)}, A)$, then *E* (*A'*) and this is *desirable* $J_{(u)}$.

So we suppose:

(8) "James" conformity with his *practical consistency d* expressed in his mental and physical behavior *h* at the time-point *i*. So we conclude:
(9) The agent disposes about the *concept of intentions, beliefs, wants.* Therefore they are not simple dispositions. We re-interpret items of behavior with respect to different *principles of act constitutions*; they are the limit of comparability and understanding of others.

I do not make the assumption that beliefs are mental dispositions. An agent has a certain belief that *p* if he has the concept about the attitudes to dispose about the propositional content of attitudes by fulfillment conditions. This supposes that some of his hypotheses and other beliefs are true and some of his actions are successful. But this is not enough because the inside of the agent is his conformity with his practical consistency as a feature not only of himselves, but also of *ourselves*. But this does not explain the *strength of our attitudes*.

In contrast to Davidson's concept of primary reasons, we do not interpret intentions, beliefs, reasons themselves as causes. This would break up our model of an intentional explanation of action. In so far the reasons like beliefs, desires, and intentions are the premises that an interpreter supposes in redescribing behavior. This is also an argument of Wright. He argues that reasons (beliefs and other attitudes) for actions are a "global fact", and such dispositions do not only exist in a specified time point; we individuate logically such reasons by agents and their verbal and other behavior.[113] This does not mean that causal features do not play any role in the analysis of actions. We have reclassified the body movement and its causal role as a component of actions. We interpret "James intentions as a mental activity" in a given case: James's act of killing Smith is caused by his activity, so Smith was killed. This activity may be thereby something that was caused by the pulling of the trigger of the pistol.

If we find out reasons to explain actions in sentences like "Peter did x because...", we give our addressee no reach information.

How we do understand what someone has done by knowing beliefs and intentions? The answer is: reasons are the premises for doing something, and from these premises we conclude the intentions of future actions.

But how do we recognize such reasons? Are reasons facts?[114] If in a given case we agree with the assertion that "Peter has shot Smith because Smith has killed his father" is true, have we then localized Peter's beliefs and intentions as reasons for his deed?

In most cases we would accept such a localization.

But what is this reason? Is it the fact that Smith has killed Peter's father?

This is not the case. Peter's reason is his thought, that is, his belief that Smith has killed his father. Then again, if Smith had not killed his father, Peter would have the same reason for his deed: his belief that Smith has killed his father. If Smith killed Peter's father, then Peter's assumption of Smith's deed is only a fact in the sense that his belief is true. If we give the following explanation: *Peter has shot Smith because Smith has killed his father, then the truth of his belief is partially fixed by the context of the explanation.* The truth of the statement has contextual presuppositions. "Peter has shot Smith because he knows that Smith has killed his father" gives us the reason for Peter's deed. This redescription of his reason is also the case if his belief is not proven in the story of the death of Peter's father. Therefore, we understand actions in the light of reasons. Yet, we take into account for all such explanations in principle: "Beliefs and desires that would rationalize an action if they caused it in the right way ... may cause it in other ways. If so, the

---

113 Wright, Normen, Werte und Handlungen. Frankfurt am Main 1994, 151.

114 Shwayder, Stratification of Behavior, "A reason ... *is a fact, the knowledge of which by an animal would explain his movements.*", 65.

action was not performed with the intention that we could have read of from the attitudes that caused it. What I despair of spelling out is the way in which attitudes must cause actions if they are to rationalize the action."[115] But the *ultimate inscrutability* of primary reasons from the interpreter's point of view is not a ground that our doings would not be evaluated as successful or unsuccessful, right or wrong.

Practical thoughts imply a generalization. The ascription of attitude goes along with generalizations because attitudes cannot be only momentary. In the following there is to say something more about this. The possibility cannot be excluded that our ex-post considerations show that the reason we ascribe to an agent was one among many other reasons. In the case of explaining actions, the antecedence entails the ascription of attitudes. The description and ascription of attitudes is a singular premise (condition) for the conclusion. A similar problem arises in the teleological explanation because it is not possible to explain any action from its end, for example, we could not explain the killing of James by the event that his death happened. A part of the singular antecedence of teleological explanations are the description of intentional behavior, like "x beliefs, desires, intents, knows". The generalizations that connect reasons and action are always hypothetical. But this is not a dramatic matter and doesn't prevent us from taking in the explanation actions in the general scheme of scientific explanation. The problem is another one: when explaining actions by beliefs and desires, the feature of desirability of the content of such attitudes comes into play from the agent's point of view, and this makes a difference to physical explanation.

Ascription of actions supposes that the offered description is intelligible and we portray the doing in such a way. This means that we ascribe actions from the perspective of a *concept of propositional attitudes of the agent* whom we want to understand. We presuppose that we know tentatively the *background theory* to make behavior intelligible. If we accept that explanation of action takes propositional attitudes in the *framework of folk psychology* or *sociology*, then we have to analyse this *framework*.[116] The answer of the question must also be an answer to the problem of the common-sense framework of individuation of intentional states and the constituents of thought, that is, "Are inten-

115 Davidson, Freedom to Act (1973), 79. In: Action and Events.
116 A.I. Goldman, Folk Psychology and Mental Concepts, ProtoSociology Vol. 14 2000: Folk Psychology, Mental Concepts and the Ascription of Attitudes. On Contemporary Philosophy of Mind, 4-24.

tional states related to private or public, abstract or concrete object?, and "What is the epistemical role of the self-knowledge (the thinker knows what he things) and the first person authority of the thinker?". The first is caused by the acquisition of knowledge from outside. This cannot be assumed a priori. Therefore situations of the acquisition of knowledge are to take into play. The problem in the theory of language and mental is whether language is learnt. The second is that first person authority means that the thinker has his authority knowing the content of his intentional states but the content is to individuate (narrow or wide content). At the same time he knows the content directly without evidence. His knowledge is authoritative in contrast to knowledge by evidence. But the problem of non-evident knowledge is the *problem of the role thinker's direct knowledge of the intentional state content.*

Understanding always means explaining something. The connection of the explanation of behavior, no matter whether linguistic or not, supposes that we are successful in ascribing propositional attitudes and describe actions as connected with intentions. Successful actions and communications are an evidence that the most part of our shared ontology is true, and therefore we speak about the same things, events, and regulations. But the observation of behavior as obvious in its causation is not a guarantee that speakers (people) are radically interpretable from the third person point of view.

We only dispose of the *concept of intention* if we are ourselves acquainted and know that intending (forming a intention) means to perform something. This goes along with that I know therefore that, for example, "I spill the coffee" myself if I identify myself with the person who is thinking this thought. We could interpret *intending* not only with respect to the relevant belief of the agent. Provided that someone intends to do something, he has certain beliefs about the way of the goal-attainment at his disposal, and he has to make decisions and form intentions also that are to satisfy. It is to explain *what* beliefs and intentions are and *how* the connection with them both leads to the consequence of an action. Practical thoughts imply intentions, but we have to distinguish between *thoughts* and *beliefs*. With this step we go on to the explanation of action as an explanation with reasons that includes different intentions.

A theory of agent cannot avoid presupposing the consistence and fulfillment set of attitudes from the side of an agent for the intelligible redescription behavior and the ascription of actions: successful action and communication are an evidence for a largely true view of the world. But this way a problem emerges. It is not enough that we optimize our agreement in truth-values in the course of interpretation. A theory of agent makes the assumption: if we know the attitudes of an agent, then we understand from our description of it the doings of this agent in a particular way; we describe its actions as such of which he assumes that they satisfy his attitudes. This is not only a matter of the individuation of the content of attitudes by the things and events which cause them. If someone intends to perform an action, then an interpreter assumes that the agent has also certain beliefs how he can reach his aim. We see that thoughts, meaning and actions do not stand alone, but have different fulfillment conditions. The answer to the question, "Why did James x?" has clarified that, for example, "James" has the disposition to act in correspondence with his practical reasoning (premises) and practical consistency. In the next step it is to show that the analysis of practical thought and an intentional explanation of action give us an interpretation of the scheme of action that is represented in a practical inference, and an answer of the validity of such reasoning shall be given.

Part II
Practical Reasoning

The origin of action—its efficient, not its final cause—is choice, and that of choice is desire and reasoning with a view to an end.

Aristotle[1]

1. Decision and the Execution of Intention

Decisions are contingent. They are not a part of nature. But they are not without any restrictions also. They must be bound or restricted, that is, they are premises for further decisions which we do not dispose about because they a premises for other decisions. Such restrictions have to be effective without the reference to rationality of decisions, its benefit, and also with respective to expectations of the members of social systems that they expect. *Decisions are distinctions that we do not only ascribe to instances which we mark as individuals (person) but also to the members of social systems.* Our common sense, and also theories of decision, establish the construction of an individual agent as an instance who decides something by his interests, reasons, motives, or whatever. This is a fictive model of ascription and a projection of an observer. Decision has a temporal structure. This structure makes the distinction between nature, social systems, and their members who decide about something. A decision has a relationship to the past and the future. At the moment when someone makes a decision, he brings about a distinction between the past and the future. The past comes to an end, and the future is not fixed at the moment of the decision. A new story begins. Therefore decisions are partially annihilations. We do not know what the future holds in store. So every decision is a new beginning and is underdetermined by the coming time. Every decision confirms that we do not know the future but that we make projections on the coming events. The unknown future is the guarantee that there are decisions. If I say that instances of individuals as models of ascription are fictions, I do not say that there are no mental (psychological) descriptions of them.[2]

---

1 Aristotle, Nicomachean Ethics. Ed. and trans. by Martin Ostwald. New York 1962, 1139a 31-33.
2 On the temporal structure of decision, see also N. Luhmann, Das Recht der

The word *intending* stands in a relation to *choose* and *decide* (Austin). It is quite obvious that the use of words like "choose", "decide", "intending" is relative. We can compare the use of these words with "to decide". Practical reasoning leads to a choice and an intention. Thereby we connect the explanation of action and practical reasoning. Decisions, like intentions, are to re-interpret as executive mental states, and there is a relation between decisions and intentional actions.[3] It is the analysans of decisions that we dispose about alternatives and we choose between these. A choice, for example, between *a* and *b* implies, in case we choose *a*, a *decision* for *a* in contrast to to *b*, and also the *intention* to do *a* and not *b*. This is to complete with the *principle of decision*.

Raz makes the assumption that decisions are not norms. He characterizes decisions in the following way:

1. to decide is to *form an intention*,
2. decisions are reached as a *result of deliberations*,
3. decisions are taken *some time before the action*, and
4. decisions are *reasons*.[4]

If we take the relationship between *decisions* and *reasons* seriously, then the analysans of decisions are *exclusionary reasons*.[5] The *principle of decision* is the following:

* People are able to generate *exclusionary reasons* for the limitation of their further deliberation to find decisions. That is: *I know what I will* not *do*; this is the limit for stopping my deliberations. *Exclusionary reasons eliminate inconsistency in the deliberation*. Therefore, the *principle of consistency* works together with the *principle of decision*. These reasons are first order reasons for any solution of practical imperatives. But that principle does not exclude that someone has no reasons for acting.

When applying this principle we make the assumption that in the case of "*a* and non-*a*" they cannot both be true. The making of decisions

Gesellschaft. Frankfurt am Main 1993, 307-10 in continuation of G. I. S. Shackle, Imagination, Formalism, and Choice. In: M. J. Rizzo (ed.) Time, Uncertainty, and Disequilibrium: Explorations in Austrian Theme. Lexington Mass. 1979, 19-31.
3 See also Mele, Springs of Action, 156-160.
4 J. Raz, Practical Reason and Norms. London 1978, 133-134.
5 Raz, Practical Reason and Norms, 129-133.

is not only a mode of arriving at an all-out judgment. The decision to do something relates intending to intentional actions. Not only goals are reasons for actions, but also the existence of my intention is conditioned by a decision. From my point of view this is the answer of the question "What is the relation between beliefs, intentions, desires and intentional action?".

If an agent begins to act, then the interpreter redescribes this given behavior under study in an incomplete way. The positive values of the descriptions, for example, the end of acting and the performances, are not to state with certain conditions. The elementary principle to limit these descriptions is the propositional expression in the sense of *it will be the case that* ... (Sellars: "So Be It" inference).

The *principle of execution intentions* and *making beliefs true* is the general orientation to interpret descriptions of action. *The essential feature of the transition of an intentional explanation in the scheme of a practical inference is the interpretation of practical premises as an expression of an intention.* The intention to do x is to interpret as the intention that someone does x. The propositio minor corresponds to the deliberation that the condition of application of the conclusion is satisfied. All intentions are to express in singular canonical form. These statements are not true or false, as Sellars argues. If someone makes a decision on the basis of certain reasons he accepts, then something is to say about the concept of preferences. If someone intends to bring about a, he has a preference for a but not for non-a. This simple *concept of preferences* goes back to Sellars. It links preferences with intentions and deliberations because decisions about what someone will do suppose a preference for doing a but not non-a. Therefore beliefs can support our preferences. These are no extensive pieces of logical information, but they are good enough for understanding the concept of preferences.

However, do we need a particular logic for evaluating practical inferences?

If, for example, "James" says "I will read T. Parsons in the afternoon", then he expresses an intention to read Parsons and not Y. Mishima in the afternoon. In this case we suppose that "James" has reasons, or even good reasons, to do that. If "James" does not read "Parsons", we cannot assert that his intention is "false", but we can say about "James" that he has not executed his intention. In this respect, a so-called logic of intention (Sellars) is a logic of execution of intentions and making attitudes true. So statements like "I shall do a" imply the overall consistency of intentions and beliefs. This shows us the general feature of the optimization of consistency of intentions and beliefs:

without such practical consistency we would misunderstand each other and could not interpret other people's behavior. The *principle of execution of intentions* and *making beliefs true* is a modified version of the *principle of continence*: "... perform the action judged best on the basis of all available relevant reasons."[6] We are able to perform such actions by practical consistency, and this is not only an empirical theory about agents. The motives for doing these are our own business. The assumption of such behavior of people means that some items of behavior are to redescribe as actions. "The falsity of a belief, or the patent wrongness of a value or desire, does not disqualify the belief or desire from providing an explanatory reason. On the other hand, beliefs and desires tell us an agent's reasons for acting only if those attitudes are appropriately related to the action as viewed by the agent. To serve as reasons for an action, beliefs and desires need not be reasonable, but a normative element nevertheless enters, since the action must be reasonable in the light of the beliefs and desires (naturally it may not be reasonable in the light of further considerations)."[7] But our reasoning is always incomplete and *there are irreducibly multiple* reasons.[8] To what extent we are successful is another matter; an interpreter can break into an agent's attitudes from his external point of view.

But the *principle of elimination of inconsistency* (practical inconsistency) by exclusionary reasons and with the application of the principle of execution is not to interpret in such a way that practical inferences commit us logically to do something. Consistency or inconsistency and the fulfillment of practical reasoning in our doings are *not* logical or a matter of logical deduction. Just this shows us *what* practical commitments are. If we decide to do something we are committed to form a respective intention; that simply means, if I am to decide to bring about something x, I am at the same time committed to intending x.[9] The *logic of intention* does not imply any normative statement like "It is right, wrong, permitted ... that p". *Wants and desires do not commit us to*

6 Davidson, How is Weakness of the Will possible (1970), 41. In: Actions and Event.
7 Davidson, Intending (1978): 84. In: Action and Events.
8 Davidson, How is 'Weakness of the Will Possible? (1970), 34. In: Action and Events, J. Nida-Rümelin, The Plurality of Good Reasons and the Theory of Practical Rationality. In: G. Preyer, G. Peter (eds.), The Contextualization of Rationality. Problems, Concepts and Theories of Rationality. Perspectives in Analytical Philosophy. New Series. Edited by G. Meggle and J. Nida-Rümelin. Paderborn 2000.
9 Aune, Reason and Action. Dordrecht 1977, 166-167.

anything, but decision does. If inconsistency in doings is obvious, then we say that a practical inconsistency of an agent is shown. He can also make mistakes in his reasoning and with actions he is not conscious of; there may even be obscure cases where he is successful with making such mistakes. But this is not a falsification that intentions and beliefs are not only primary dispositions to practical thoughts but concepts of reasoning that we express in the form "I will do *a*".

2. Practical Inference

In correspondence with Aristotle's *Nicomachean Ethics, book 3,* practical thinking is to interpret as a *decision.* Such thinking is a kind of deliberation including choice. The difference between theoretical and practical thinking is one of the subject. In *book 7* he has analyzed practical syllogism. In Greek, practical inferences mean a practical reasoning which is such that it leads from certain conditions in some sequences to the doing of a particular action here and now. The action is caused by the reasoning from the agent's side. The content of desire and belief is expressed in the premises of the argument and the action is the conclusion of practical inferences. Practical reasoning is the kind of mental transition that does not involve choice; many interpreters would say: not involve decision. With the word *proairesis,* he does not mean an act of choice. The best translation of this word is "will" because a choice entails stricto sensu a deliberation between alternatives. Provided that someone supposes there is only a "one way trip" to attain his goals, so he will act but not deliberate any alternatives. Therefore deliberating about means does not really enter into the practical syllogism, where belief and desire lead directly to action. Decisions and choices are in fact forms of intentions, but not all intentions are born by decisions. This is only the case if decisions are formed in a particular way, such is, provided they are formed by the process of deliberation. This is meant by the Greek word *proairesis.* Aristotle himself does not speak of a particular act of decision which connects the *deliberation about means* to a desirable *goal* and *actions.* But the reasoning does not simply work in an Aristotelian sense, and it is not obvious that the logic of the reasoning corresponds to the causation of action. Aune shows

"(a) his (Aristotle) syllogistic account of deductive inference is insufficient to deal with the varieties of deductive inference that we recognize today;

(b) his account of deliberation is inadequate for dealing with what is now known as "decision-making under uncertainty," where probabilistic considerations are crucial; and

(c) his account of the sort of premises or conclusions that moves us to act is inadequately developed. Filling in these inadequacies is, as I see it, the major task of anyone concerned the logic (broadly speaking) of practical inference."[10]

The intentional explanation in the last chapter has involved a practical premise in accordance with our practical thinking.

What is the problem when applying the *intentional explanation* to *practical inferences* in respect of the information of such inferences in principle?

(1) *A* will/intends to bring about *E* or prevent *E*.
(2) *A* believes that he will bring about *E* or prevent *E*
by doing *a*.
(3) Therefore, he will do *a*.

(1) expresses an intention and a preference for *E*;
(2) expresses a cognitive attitude, and it is assumed that *A* can really do *a*;
(3) could be interpretable as a decision and that *A* tries or begins to do something.

But (3) merely says that *A* will do *a*; and at the same time a reasonable person certainly does not do everything that will bring about an end that he desires. The variable "*A*" can be substituted with "I", "names" or other descriptions with which a person refers to himself or a group. *The inference describes the transition from an intention and cognitive attitudes to decisions, and the actions are consequences of such decisions.* Inference is not deductive. It is a (rational) maxim. But it can transit to a deductive inference:

(1) $C_1, C_2, \ldots C_n$
(2) Under the conditions $C_1, C_2, \ldots C_n$ a rational agent x decides to bring about the action *a* or in all cases $C_1, C_2, \ldots C_n$ if x intends q and believes that p is causally necessary for q, he will do p.

10 Aune, Formal Logic and Practical Reasoning. Theory of Decision 20 1986, 6.

(3) x is a rational agent A.
(4) A decides to do the action a[11].

I have argued that practical thought implies a generalization and a confirmation of the agent's hypothesis. The questionable relation is of p and q to a. This leads us to the problem:

What is the role of generalizations in the universal premise of a practical inference?

The necessity of a general law like a statement in the premise (2) is called *Ducasse-sentence*.[12] The question is:

What does such knowledge tell us about an agent's reasons?

Davidson has distinguished between strict laws and rules of thumb. Also we assume that beliefs and desires cause actions, consequently such explanations are themselves not serious laws. Laws which relate mental and physical events cannot be reduced to physical concepts and laws of physics. If we have enough information about the beliefs and desires of an agent, we can also extract a general knowledge, and this makes our explanation of reason informative. Such knowledge tells us nothing about an agent's particular reasons. But it is helpful to fit it in the scientific explanation. Davidson makes a difference between *laws* as *true universally quantified statements* which are supported by counterfactuals and are confirmed by their instances and the *application of laws without ceteris paribus clauses*. *Strict laws* do not contain singular terms referring to particular objects, locations and time. They do not use causal tendencies, potentialities, and dispositions and do not use phrases like "other things being equal", and "under normal conditions". Non-strict laws explain causally in respect of *special explanatory interests*. Anomalous monism is reasoned by this distinction. Davidson argues that explanation implies empirical generalization (Hempel) and a law plus other premises explains us the events that had

11 D. Wunderlich, Studien zur Sprechakttheorie. Frankfurt am Main 1976, 260; on the weak or strong conditionals which are expressed in the premise of the practical inference (2) *A* believes that he brings about *E* or prevents *E* by doing *a*, 264-72.

12 C. J. Ducasse, Nature, Mind, and Death. Illinois 1951. On the Ducasse-sentence, see Davidson, Law and Cause (1995), 209-12. In: Truth, Language, and History. Oxford 2005. He argues that Ducasse confuses both 1. particular events with events of the same type, and 2. sufficient conditions are to apply to events and to sentences about, and descriptions of, events. Davidson, Law and Cause (1995), 209-10. In: Truth, Language, and History.

to happen. Such laws have no application to explanations by primary reasons because laws of all mankind redescribe information how people may act under certain circumstance but tell us nothing about individual cases.[13]

However, the question is:

Are practical inferences explanatory arguments? What are the limits of the integration of explaining action in scientific explanations?

Anscombe argued that a practical inference is not deductive. From her point of view, a practical inference corresponds to a practical reasoning, and the conclusion of such inference corresponds to a judgment, that is, *the action itself is desirable or reasonable and does not only have a desirable property*. Another problem she emphasized is that the universal premise in practical inferences like, for example, "One must always keep a promise", does not cause a particular action. *It expresses only an intention, a wish (want), or a belief, which are fulfilled by any action*. For Aristotle, the practical inference gives *necessary conditions* for an action, but there are well-known cases in our everyday life like not holding our promises.[14]

Aristotle and also other philosophers assume that *practical reasoning describes actual mental processes*.[15] We may argue that intentions (wants) and beliefs prompt practical reasoning, and that it begins with them. But states of believing and wants are themselves *no* premises in an inference and the act *a*; for example, raising the arm is no conclusion of an inference. The act may be produced from a complex state of believing, and this act may show a justified relationship to such state, but the step from a state of believing to an action is not an inference that we evaluate as logically valid or not.[16] Also in case (2) is a necessary and sufficiency condition, the inference does not express a logical commitment for the agent. With intentions, the same is the case. They may prompt a practical reasoning, but such reasoning does not commit

13 Davidson, Problems in the Explanation of Action (1987), 110-16. In: Problems of Rationality, Hempel on Explaining Action (1976), 273-75. In: Action and Event. Oxford 1980. On critique on Davidson's distinction, J. Kim, Psychophysical Laws, 194-236. In: Supervenience and Mind. Selected Philosophical Essays. Oxford 1993, Rogler, Preyer, Materialismus, anomaler Monismus und mentale Kausalität: 50-53.

14 Anscombe, Intention, 57-67. On a summary of Anscombe's turn Davidson, Aristotle's Action (2001), 283-85. In: Truth, Language, and History, Oxford 2005.

15 On critique, Anscombe, Intention, 79-80.

16 On this problem, Aune, Reason and Action, 119-123

us to doing a particular action. Therefore, practical inferences are *no* explanatory arguments. They describe the intention, desire and belief of an agent, that is, why he brings about *E*, but not his factual reasoning, and the inference is not a prediction.

This interpretation is different to Wright's distinction between practical inferences in the *first* and *third person*.[17] For Wright, the inferences in the first person express a commitment of an agent and they are practical in the sense of Aristotle, whereas the corresponding third person inference does not have this property. Such inferences of third person are a statement of an "objective practical necessity", and it is theoretical. In this case, the validity of inference leads to the verification of descriptions of actions as an intentional doing and not merely to a statement that *a* is a result of, for example, moving my hand.[18] It is obvious that the so-called *necessity* of the inference is only *hypothetical*. Such inferences can be false, and the agent is not committed to any action. The conclusion does not have any practical force. *Therefore an agent is not logically committed do something by the premises, even if they are fulfilled or if he accepts them.* So the conclusion or the good reasons have no practical force or do not express any logical commitment or necessity. The interpretation of practical inferences leads to a problem in principle: "Any serious theory for predicting actions on the basis of reasons must find a way of evaluating the relative force of various desires and beliefs in the matrix of decision; it cannot take as its starting point the refinement of what is to be expected from a single desire. The practical syllogism exhausts its role in displaying an action as falling under one reason; so it cannot be subtilized into a reconstruction of practical reasoning, that involves the weighing of competing reasons. The practical syllogism provides a model neither for a predictive science of action nor for a normative account of evaluative reasoning."[19] Therefore practical inferences cannot answer us a question like, "Shall

---

17 Wright, Practical Inference. Philosophical Review 72 1963, 172, 168-69. The same is found in: Wright, Explanation and Understanding, Ithaca, N.Y. 1971: On Wright, see G. Meggle, 166-171, on understanding actions and practical inferences and Wright's modification of his earlier approach, 178, 200. In: Wright, Normen, Werte und Handlungen, Frankfurt am Main 1994.

18 Wright, Erklären und Verstehen (1971), Frankfurt am Main 1974: 102-103, on Wright see Aune, Reason and Action, 119-123.

19 Davidson, Actions, Reasons, and Causes (1963), 16. In: Actions and Events.

I do what I want to do?", "Shall I do what I ought to do?", "Shall I do what is the best, most reasonable thing to do?" or, "Shall I do what I have just 'told' myself to do?". If someone has a good reason for doing something, he is not committed do it. Reasons tell us that something is reasonable, but they do not logically force us to perform any action. Shwayder argues that practical inferences are no arguments. He calls such statements *doxastic inference* as a guide of deliberation. The difference between these two inferences is that the doxastic ones have true or false premises and inferences.[20]

But the question what *practical commitments* are must be answered.

This leads us to the relationship between decisions and intentions and between intentions and intentional actions.

Conventionally we name this *deliberation*, which *ends in a decision*, *practical thinking*. Such reasoning is to distinguish from theoretical thinking by the fact that such reasons lead to a *decision* or choice but not to a *statement*. It is unimportant whether a decision is a choice or not; and also in case that such decisions are not deducted in this way, there is no question of formal validity of reasons for action in the sense of deontic logic because the conclusion cannot be justified by its premises. Therefore, the conclusion has not the force of a reason that we have to accept: the validity is only hypothetical and does not logically commit us to do anything. Yet, the conclusion of a practical inference is always valid in a formal way if we deduct it from our deliberation about this reasoning. But such conclusions are not helpful for the "weighing of competing reasons". So the statement of validity of practical inferences is not to distinguish from our *formal logic of ordinary assertoric inference*.[21] Both conclusions apply the same general principles: so all valid practical inferences correspond to valid inferences of the formal assertoric logic. The correspondence is shown by the following example:

(1) I (we) will bring about E.
(2) If I (we) do not x, so I cannot bring about E.
(3) Therefore, I (we) will do x.

20 Shwayder, The Stratification of Behavior, 94-96.
21 Sellars, Thought and Action. In: K. Lehrer (ed.), Freedom and Determinism. New York 1966, Science and Metaphysics. London 1968, Action and Events. Nous 7 1973. On Sellars with some modifications, Aune, Reason and Action, 144-58.

If the argument is valid, then we interpret the premise (2) in such a way that it implies

(4) if I (we) shall bring about E, so I shall do x

We interpret the word *shall* in the sense that it refers to a future event. In this case the words "I (we) will . . ." as an expression of a *volition* (an intention) and "I (we) shall . . ." as an *indicative* are not *logically* and *semantically* different. Although 'I will do A' is an expression of volition while 'I shall do A' is a mere future indicative, both describe the same action on the subject's part, and for this reason they may be regarded as logically indistinguishable: the volitional attitude expressed by an utterance of the first is not part of its propositional content. The attitude expressed by 'but' differs from the attitude expressed by 'and,' but as sentence connectives both the words are rightly represented by the same logical symbol. We may hear the word differently, but they both have semantically (logically) comparable values like "p and q" and "p but q" or even "p although q."[22] The attitude expressed by *but* differs from the attitude expressed by *and*, but as sentence connectives both words are rightly represented by the *same logical symbol*. The conclusion (3) is deducted from (1) and (4) and evaluated by the theorem of modus ponendo ponens.[23] The canonical structure of "I (we) shall..." and "It shall be that p" have fulfillment conditions as semantic values. The relevant logic is the formal logic of ordinary assertoric inference that we use for the evaluation of the premises. If the values of these conditions are not identical, then one must know whether they are not the same values of these conditions.

The conclusion in a *practical inference* is the *description* of what is implied by the premises, that is, the description is given in reference to a rule and so to a deliberation. But practical reasoning can also appear in many non-syllogistic forms, particularly forms that involve a choice between alternatives. This was Aristotle's proposal in his *Nikomachean Ethics*. Only in the case, if the disposition to do something is given and

22 "Will" and "shall" are not logical words, and a logical counterpart is not necessary. On a semi-formal treatment of inferences, Aune, Formal Logic and Practical Reasoning. Theory of Decision 20 1986, 301-20.

23 This is quite conform to the interpretation of practical inferences of Davidson, Aune, Sellars, Rescher, Rationalität. Würzburg 1993, 239. We use the classical logic evaluating the validity of practical inferences. See also Aune, Formal Logic and Practical Reasoning.

the belief that the conditions of execution of our intentions are satisfied, then an intentional action would be done. Yet also in this case it may be that our intent is going wrong, for example, Hamlet kills Polonius but that is not his prior intention. The scheme of practical inferences describes in this extent which action can be, *not* need be, a result of a reasonable deliberation. But the scheme is not a procedure to evaluate actions, nor is it a method to decide what I ought to do. It may be provided that an agent has a certain desire and a belief and also the conditions are given to cause an action, but a radical interpreter cannot discover the causation of actions by attitudes in particular as, for example, in the case of lunatic internal causal chains of actions, the climber-example. In Aristotle's concept of deliberation it is misleading that he thinks that the conclusion is an action. On the contrary: it is a statement and not an action. Also practical inferences are not a question of acting but of thinking. An action may satisfy a practical inference, but it is not possible that actions constitute any inference. With practical reasoning we have to take into account that a desire and a belief may in some cases cause an action, but in other cases both lead only to a prima facie statement.[24] This cannot be eliminated. It is also not to exclude that from true premises of practical inferences a contradiction follows because, for example, I hold my promise given Pia to be punctual but I break my word given Maria that I will never meet my old girlfriend: "We can hardly expect to learn whether an action ought to be performed simply from the fact that it is both prima facie right and prima facie wrong"[25]. Time after time there is a gap between theory and practise, opinion and action. And this is also true if we sympathize with the wisdom of Zen-Buddhism that there ought to be no breath between thinking and doing. This is in harmony with the characteristic feature of incontinence also: "What is special in incontinence is that the agent cannot understand himself: he recognizes, in his own intentional behavior, something essentially surd."[26] Therefore there is no absolute incontinence except what we know about it in every day life. It echoes Aristotle's thought that the nasty in the world is caused by a weak will, that is, a lack of virtue.

24 Davidson, How is Weakness of the Will Possible? (1970), 32. In: Actions and Events.

25 Davidson, How is Weakness of the Will Possible? (1970), 37. In: Actions and Events.

26 Davidson, How is Weakness of the Will Possible? (1970), 42. In: Actions and Events.

How far can the redescription of the belief that the conditions of a practical inference (thought) are satisfied be explained by the attributive adverb "prima facie", like a prima facie judgment of "correct", "obligatory", "satisfied", "good", and so on?

This leads us back again to the role of the *Ducasse-sentence* in practical inferences. *Davidson argues that prima facie judgments correspond to evaluative attitudes but not a universally quantified conditional.* From this judgment we cannot infer deductive inferences. In particular it is not to conclude that an action is correct or obligatory, whatever.[27] He identifies a problem of the validity of practical inferences in principle. A theory of practical reason cannot detach conclusions about what is desirable (or better).[28] Therefore we need a *stronger* judgment.[29]

Yet, how far do our strongest beliefs that we express in all-out judgments cause our intentional actions?

The answer leads us to the explanation of action as an interplay between desires, beliefs and intentions with respect to the desirable content of an action, that is: "When an intention is formed we go from a stage in which we perceive, or imagine that we perceive, the attraction and drawbacks of a course of action to a stage in which we commit ourselves to act. This may be just another pro-attitude, but an intention, unlike other desires or pro-attitudes, is not merely conditional or prima facie. If it is to produce an action, it cannot be simply an appreciation that some good would come of acting in a certain way."[30] From such strongest belief as a premise, an interpreter redescribes the intention (explanatory redescription) in terms of consequences described as intended. The redescription answers the question, "Why did you do that?". But the intentional action may also be caused by other attitudes. Therefore, the explanatory redescription is not a factual description of the deliberation of the agent under study. Yet, unconditional judgments always lead to a decision to do something. Maybe we have a desire or a belief and do not act accordingly: but we cannot decide to do something without beginning to act in a certain way. This is a differ-

---

27 Davidson, How is Weakness of the Will Possible? (1970), 36-39. In: Actions and Events.

28 Davidson, How is Weakness of the Will Possible? (1970), 37. In: Actions and Events.

29 Davidson claims to show that practical thinking is an illusion, see II 2. (a), in this book.

30 Davidson, Problems in the Explanation of Action (1987), 107. In: Problems of Rationality.

ence to Davidson's account because, for him, decisions are prima facie judgments that are not directly associated with actions. For him, the desirable feature of an action is no sufficient condition to perform such actions. The practical inference shows us the reason for which someone has acted but it does not show that the action is desirable or what the factual reasoning was (it is a fragment).

In sum: we find the deductive features of practical reasoning within the framework of the formal logic of ordinary assertoric inference (principles). Practical reasoning ends in a choice and is not at all deductive. The evaluation of choices must take in degrees of beliefs (subjective probabilities) and systems of preferences. This is a limitation of the domain of formal logic because this is not given us by logic itself. The analysis of intending by all-out judgments is to re-interpret that the realization of an intention will happen only by our decision to do something: when deciding in favor of something, we form our intention of doing something. *I decide to bring about* x, *I intend to do so; I am not merely committed to having this intention.*[31] In this context the prior intention is significant because intending is forming a decision by our strongest beliefs as exclusionary reasons. For Davidson, however, we could also come to all-out judgments without such modes as deciding, choosing, and deliberating to arrive at them.[32]

3. The Humean Theory of Motivation

What is the relationship between beliefs and the motivation of actions? What role do our beliefs play for the motivation of actions? What are intentional or voluntary actions? Are actions only motivated by desires?

The answer to these questions leads us back to Hume's theory of motivation. Hume's theory of practical reasoning is not different from Aristotle's. Both agree about the means-end scheme: ends are determined by passions and reason determines the means. A Humean theory of motivation is: "The dogma from philosophical psychology is that any complete specification of even a prima facie reason for action must make reference to the potential agent's desires or possible desires. The idea crudely is that even any prima facie reason for doing something will make reference, in the antecedent of a conditional, to

31 This is emphasized by B. Aune in his comments to the chapter.
32 Davidson, Intending (1978), 99. In: Actions and Events.

the potential agent's actual or possible desires—'if you desire that...,
then, prima facie, you have a reason to make it the case that...'. Such a
reason becomes the potential agent's own reason, a motivating reason
for him, if he has, and recognizes himself to have, the desire specified in
the antecedent of the conditional. If the agent performs the appropriate
action, and does so for that reason, then he does so because he has, and
recognizes himself to have, that desire. It is just that the prima facie motivating reason was, in the circumstances (including his other desires),
a sufficient reason for acting; it sufficed for action."[33] For Hume, our
reasoning is unable to motivate our actions. It can only indirectly cause
them. Our motivation to do anything is only caused by desire (a passion) as a necessary condition.[34] He insists on the general distinction
between desires and beliefs as reasons and intentions or other attitudes
as motives. For this account, descriptions of actions show us desires
that are of original existence. In the case of conflict between desires, the
stronger desire is going to win and causes the action. But if someone
brings about something, we presuppose that he has also beliefs about
how he might put his desire into effect. However, it may be that I have
the desire to drink vinegar, but I never do it. We can induce to do something by reasons, beliefs, and desire. With Hume's theory we cannot
explain our practical commitments because all actions are caused by
certain sensory perceptions like, for example, getting hungry, being
thirsty, and so on, which correspond to undirected desires. Such states
cannot be controlled by the agent. Beliefs come into play if undirected
desires are converted in directed ones. For Hume, our descriptive beliefs
(epistemic beliefs) are the slaves of our desires, and all of our conative
attitudes are to explain by non-rational and undirected basic-desires,
which take descriptive beliefs into play. Surely there are many cases in
which this is so, but this is not the basis of practical thinking in general.
An agent can always act contrary to his desire, for example, he satisfies
a social expectation or a normative belief, and it is not to exclude that
beliefs modify our desire; and there are surely many cases which show
that it is irrational to act by our strongest desires. H. G. Frankfurt is
right when he argues that people have the capability of taking in into

---

33 M. Platts, Morality and the End of Desire, 73. In: Platt (ed.), Reference, Truth and Reality. Essays on the Philosophy of Language. London
   1980.
34 On critique on the Humean theory J. Nida-Rümelin, Strukturelle Rationalität. Ein philosophisches Essay über praktische Vernunft. Stuttgart
   2001, 21-38.

their wants also desires of the second level. It is a difference whether "I desire something" or whether "I desire that I desire something". He calls that *volition*: "Someone has a desire of the second order either when he wants simply to have a certain desire or when he wants a certain desire to be his will".[35] In the latter situation, we have a volition of a second order. *Second order desires presuppose the capacity for reflective self-evaluation.* Therefore we can conclude that deliberations and choices in respect for alternatives are naturalistically underdetermined.[36] This underdetermination is essential for the freedom humans have. But it is not disputed that empirical psychology can explain us some token of basic desire.[37]

Hume gives us no answer to the question:

Why is a desire necessary for an intentional action?

It may be that I have a disposition to drink alcohol but I never do it. Contrary to Hume, my assumption is that our decision and intending are caused only by the requirements of a given situation. Reasons can motivate our actions. Intentional actions may be projected by the system of attitudes and the complex of desire, but they are only born by *decision*. A desire only does not exhaust a decision. Also the tokens of desires and descriptive beliefs do not necessarily trigger actions. It cannot be excluded that people frustrate their desire in principle.

How is the relationship between wanting, choosing, deciding, intending to determine? What is the principle to evaluate the performance of actions?

We are confronted with Davidson's *principle of motivational strength* that he hold as self-evident; I will call it the *problem of motivation.*

Davidson gives the following solution of the problem. For him, the motivation condition is:

Principle 1: If an agent wants to do x more that he wants to do y and he believes himself free to do either x or y, then he will intentionally do x if he does either x or y intentionally.

---

35 H. Frankfurt, Freedom of the Will and the Concept of the Person. Journal of Philosophy Vol. 68 1 1971, 10. Nida-Rümelin, Strukturelle Rationalität, 25-33. On Frankfurt see Nida-Rümelin, Über menschliche Freiheit, Stuttgart 2005, 80-92, on a summary on desires, desires second level and beliefs, 86.

36 On this concept, Nida-Rümelin, Über menschliche Freiheit, 92-94.

37 A particular problem are *irresistible desires*; see Mele, Springs of Action, 86-97.

The second principle is connected with the motivation or wanting:

Principle 2: If an agent judges that it would be better to do x than to do y, the he wants to do x more than he wants to do y.

Davidson concludes from both principles that the following:

Principle 3: There are incontinent actions.[38]

is false.

What is the problem of this answer of motivational strength?

From my point of view, *Principle 1* is relevant and well-known for all proposals which take in intentional attitudes in the framework of causal explanations of action. In this context we come upon to the background presumptions applying the principle of elimination of inconsistency, of execution of intentions, making true or fulfilling attitudes. The ultimate motives of agents cannot be researched. It also may be that the agent does not know them. There are limits of understanding. But the explanatory redescription of behavior as intentional always explains the doings of others from our own perspective. It would not be possible to explain behavior as action if the distinction between intentional and non-intentional action was not made. If this was not the case, we could not ascribe responsibility to intentional doings, and at the some time we could not ascribe to someone that he/she is a member of a social system.

All this shows us the problem that cannot be eliminated theoretically: it is not ex ante to exclude that a desire and a belief may in some cases cause an action, but in other cases the result of our deliberation is a prima facie judgment. We are confronted with that: beliefs about the conditions of satisfaction on the application of practical inferences cannot be explained by prima facie judgments of "satisfied", "good", or "correct". A stronger judgment is required. With a practical conclusion we can state an intention, but we with it we cannot grasp the factual reasoning that we claim to explain. Therefore, the validity of practical reasoning is not valid in itself but by a stronger judgment. Such judgment can be formed also without a practical reasoning.

38 Davidson, How is Weakness of the Will Possible (1970), 23. In: Actions and Events. Mele argues that *Principle 1* is wrong, Mele, Springs of Action, 46-85.

Now we can answer the question of the beginning of the chapter, "What is the problem when applying the intentional explanation to practical inferences in principle?"

The practical inference does not tell us anything about the desirability of an action. Nor does it tell us anything about the agent's commitments. But it informs us about a reason and the intention the agent has. In sum, we are confronted with the problem that an ascription of intentions, like all other attitudes, presupposes the application of the principle of epistemic justice; and this lead us back to the Third Dogma of Empiricism. This is valid also in cases when our intentions are going wrong. At least they have to appear reasonable. Yet, an interpreter is not successful to discover in particular how an agent comes from his prima facie reasons to the conclusion that an action is desirable in principle. If people do not act in conformity with their best reasoning, their weakness of the will must be explained, or they are prevented from acting in consistence with their reasoning only. In this point we cannot avoid agreeing with Aristotle's sentence: *virtue, then, is a disposition governing our choice.*

4. Evaluative Attitude

(i) The Extent of the Unified Theory

> The question of the objectivity of moral judgments, or the nature of moral disputes is, then, as much a question about how the content of moral judgments is determined as it is a question about the nature and source of moral values.
>
> D. Davidson[39]

Davidson's view is that among the relations of propositional attitudes (thoughts) one must also add relations between beliefs and evaluative attitudes. Creatures have only beliefs when they also have desires. Not only beliefs but also evaluative attitudes like desires, intentions, moral convictions, obligations etc. are propositional in nature and these attitudes affect and are oblivious by behavior. Therefore beliefs, desires, values, hopes of endings conspire to cause, rationalize, and explain intentional actions in principle. Speakers express *value-commitments* in utterances about what is desirable, correct, right, and so on. We express

39 Davidson, The Objectivity of Values (1995), 43. In: Problems of Rationality.

such commitments in *prescriptions* like desirable, correct, ought to be done, or with the use of *evaluative expressions* like good, cruel, boring, generous, and so on. These expressions are used in circumstances where we utter advice and recommendations. We refer to value-commitments also to ascribe reasons of actions, for example, he has no reason to do something because he was not committed, for example, he has not promised something, he has signed the contract, and so on.

Is the concept of intelligibility of attitudes also to apply to evaluative attitudes? Is it methodologically possible to show a parallel between the attribution of non-evaluative and evaluative attitudes?

The obvious leading question is:

How it is it possible that the relation between a person and a sentence he desires to be true is extensional, assumed we have the description of the person and the sentence, and at the same time the words expressed the relation cannot be reduced to extensional concepts?

Davidson's extent of the Unified Theory is also applied to evaluative attitudes. He does not dispute that value judgments are intrinsically motivational, subjective, emotive, projective, like Hume, Bentham, Hare, Stevenson, Blackburn, and others have argued, but it is a general mistake to think that value judgments rule out objectivity.

How is the theory of interpretation and the partial external individuation of the content of attitudes connected with the objectivity of value judgments? How it is reasoned that values are just as objective like beliefs without that they have a positive ontological status: values are pseudo-entities?

The connection between cognitive and evaluative attitudes is curried out from the radical interpretation point of view because the same *sentences* are objects of beliefs and desires. The key relations are attitudes toward sentences. Embracing, accepting and holding true are not speech acts. But beliefs are too special for unification, and he refers to *what an agent judges or holds* basically.[40] It is the claim of radical interpretation that its assumptions are not unnoticed. Davidson's turn is not absolutely new that embracing the sentence, for example, "It would be good if you are punctual" is like wanting or desiring "It would be good if your are punctual" is true. But at the same kind it is an asymmetry between believing a sentence to be true and desiring that the sentence be true. The first does not entail the latter. Just this connects the procedures with evaluative judgments because, if beliefs and meaning conspire, it

40 Davidson, How is Weakness of the Will Possible? (1970), 45. In: Action and Events.

goes along with the circumstance that also beliefs, meaning, and desire are not to sort out. We break in this circle with the contrast between the attitudes of belief and of desire as directed to the *same sentences* whose interpretation is not known at the beginning. When we recognize from the choices of a speaker his preferences that a significant of his uttered sentences is true, then we have a total theory which interprets the respective sentences and we pair to them beliefs and also desires, that is, if the sentences are understood it is no problem to specify their propositional content to beliefs and desires. It is the shared frame of reference only within which differences among people about beliefs, desires, and valuations occur. The circumstances of the arrangement of values in this framework are relative to space-temporal situations and to the customs of the members of social systems. This is not a popular relativism but ties the analysis of values to the situation within which intelligible redescription takes place and their assumptions the interpreter makes. The situation and also the assumption may change, but we do not dispose about them absolutely. Yet, the assumptions themselves are not foundational in character and are not transcendental in any way.

The *Davidson-view* does not only argue for a holism of belief and meaning but also for cognitive and evaluative attitudes. The *externalistic turn* takes up also the theory of value judgments because both the objects of beliefs and values are caused by objects which are common to both the speaker and the interpreter: *values are rooted to things*.[41] The objects of all attitudes including values are the objects which caused them and just these are the same (similar) objects. Therefore, knowing what value someone has is only to recognize in a common framework, and this is a condition of interpretation. In sum: *Someone who has an emotion like being honored about the visit of his colleague must be an emotion that is consistent which his own beliefs and values.* Ultimately, the participation of people in the common ground of their doing is a condition of interpreting evaluative attitudes, that is, a shared *way of life* exists.[42] This is the basic connection between language and evaluation from Davidson's point of view.

---

41 Davidson, Objectivity of Values (1995), 51. In: Problems of Rationality. See also Expressing Evaluation (1984), Appendix: Objectivity and Practical Reasoning (2000), 19-37, 52-57. In: Problems of Rationality. On Davidson's concept of value judgment Preyer, Evaluative Attitudes. In: J. Malpas (ed.), Dialogues with Davidson. Cambridge MA. 2011.

42 Davidson, Expressing Evaluation (1984), 37. In: Problems of Rationality.

The application of guidelines of the interpretation of cognitive to the evaluative attitudes leads us to our own central value standards, the norms of consistency and of what is valuable in itself. The same general line is the externalistic individuation of the content of the uttered sentences. These standards are the basic of the interpersonal comparison of values we cannot dispose about, and that we suppose for our decisions and choices. The comparison of values comes into play within the procedure of radical interpretation because necessarily the attribution of propositional attitudes takes in such comparison. Necessarily, the interpreter matches his own values in the procedure. From the *Davidson-view*, something is wrong with the standard picture of interpersonal comparison of values when it is argued that we firstly decide about what the interests of person are, and that secondly we compare the strength of it and thirdly on this basis we decide about what to do. For Davidson, there is no reason to establish an interpersonal basis of comparison because *we already have it.*[43] Therefore we can make a clear distinction between the interpersonal comparison and the *normative statement* which is its basis. The basis of such a statement is the norm of consistency and we do not choose what is valuable in itself. This directs and explains our choice.

I agree with the *Davidson-view* in that the connection between language and evaluation is a fundamental one; but I will modify his view of value judgment and take another turn. He takes in consideration that there is no simple connection between the basic preferences for the truth of different sentences and at the same time the judgment about values which would be realized if the sentences were true. The meaning of the evaluative word like, for example, good, ought to be, obligatory, and others we use in judgments is not the same. I argue in the following that the normative statement is to exchange with the weaker principle of tolerance as a hypothetic imperative of the ascription of attitudes.

I

---

43 Davidson, The Interpersonal Comparison of Values (1986), 59-74. In: Problems of Rationality.

(ii) Cognitive and Evaluative Attitudes

> *The same sentences are the objects of both belief and desire: this reinforces the claim that the interpretation of the evaluative attitudes proceeds along the same general lines as the interpretation of the cognitive attitudes.*
>
> D. Davidson[44]

Davidson's view claims to show that this is the case.

What is the difference between evaluative and non-evaluative attitudes, and how do they work together?

The *parallel* of cognitive and evaluative attitudes is reasoned thereby because normally speakers can make a certain difference between the own evaluative attitudes and such of other people. I call this the *principle of tolerance* to concede also different evaluative attitudes. My preference to hold something as good need not be similar to that of other people, but I am free to be tolerant to others within more or less narrow or wide borders. So the ascription of evaluative attitudes depends on my *own* evaluative beliefs in all cases of reasoned ascriptions of such attitudes. Therefore it is not to exclude that there are different value-standards in principle. In contrast to that they are, for Davidson, not freely chosen. It is worth mentioning C. L. Stevenson in this context. For him, the theory of meaning of evaluative (moral) words does not commit us to particular moral beliefs, and the reasons we have for value judgments and moral beliefs do not stand in a logical relationship to the inferences we conclude. Furthermore it is not to exclude that the disagreement about moral statements is *boundless*.[45]

But could we adjust evaluative attitudes in the case of inconsistence and counter examples? Is the meaning of plausibility of evaluative and non-evaluative attitudes the same?

We could answer these questions for instance with a criticism of the realism as a *semantics of evaluative attitudes*. Realism is a strategy in semantics. It prescribes to apply truth-conditions for the interpretation of certain assertions. For the ascriptions of values and also the understanding of evaluative attitudes, the application of realism is of a particular interest. The application can be debated independently of its validity as a doctrine in semantics. Realism of values is: "Moral judgments are viewed as factually cognitive, as presenting claims about the world which can be assessed (like any then factual beliefs) as true

44 Davidson, The Interpersonal Comparison of Values (2004), 71. In: Problems of Rationality.

45 C.L. Stevenson, Ethic and Language. New York 1944.

or false, and whose truth of falsity claims about the world."[46] "The realist treats evaluative judgments as descriptions of the world whose literal significance (viz. truth-conditions) makes no reference, or generally makes no reference, to human desires, needs, wants or interests."[47] *Moral realism* is a critique of Humean theory of motivation. The realism of ascription values argues consequently that evaluative and non-evaluative beliefs are relative. A realism of values asserts an alignment of evaluative with non-evaluative beliefs. So we describe the intelligibility (rationality) of evaluative beliefs in the same way like non-evaluative attitudes. Moral realism argues that moral reality is independent of our moral beliefs. Moral properties are genuine properties of things and actions.[48] The problem is whether valuing is interpreted as desiring and whether beliefs can in themselves be practical. With moral utterances I do not express a (subjective) attitude, for example, that I detest something (emotivistic interpretation). Such utterances are not expressions of passion (expressionistic interpretation) only and I give no advice on the utterances (recommendation) (prescriptionistic interpretation). If I believe that it is immoral to murder Turkish women and girls in Solingen (Germany), this is an objective belief. Yet, without emotions such beliefs cannot take effect. There is no contradiction between the emotiveness of the utterance and its objectivity.[49]

46 M. Platts, Ways of Meaning. An Introduction to a Philosophy of Language. London 1979, 243.

47 Platts, Moral Reality and the End of Desire. In: Platts (eds.), Truth and Reality. Essay on the Philosophy of Language. London 1980, 73.

48 See on this account, for example, also J. McDowell, Are Moral Requirements Hypothetical Imperatives?: 77-95. In: McDowell (ed.) Mind, Value, and Reality. Cambridge 1998, D. McNaughton, Moral Vision. Oxford 1988, D. O. Brink, Moral Realism and the Sceptical Arguments from Disagreement and Queerness. Australian Journal of Philosophy 62 1984: 111-25 J. Dancy, Moral Realism. Oxford 1993, J.J. Thompson, G. Harman, Moral Realism and Moral Objectivity. Cambridge Mass. 1996. On an overview on both positions, A. Kulenkampff, F. Siebelt, Noncognitivist might tell a Moral Realist. ProtoSociology. An International Journal of Interdisciplinary Research, Vol. 14 2000: Folk Psychology, Mental Concepts and the Ascription of Attitudes. On Contemporary Philosophy of Mind, 355-77. On an alternative to internalism (non-cognitivism) and externalism (cognitivism), J. Nida-Rümelin, Über menschliche Freihei*t*, Stuttgart 2005, 54-5.

49 See Nida-Rühmelin, Ethische Essays, Frankfurt am Main 2002, 17. This is well in harmony with Davidson's view.

But what argument is opposed to moral realism? Why is the descriptive use and the specification of evaluative words like "good", "wrong", "bad" not to analyze semantically like descriptive concepts that we specify in the case of predication ascription in assertions?

Surely, we make in general the assumption that the verification of certain empirical properties is satisfied for the validation of evaluative and prescriptive predications. The verification evaluates something as "good" or "bad" with descriptive characterizations. A speaker who justifies such predication, for example, a value-judgment, has to show that the evaluated thing satisfied certain properties like the worth or worthless of something. If we suppose that a speaker would completely justify his evaluation with this specification and the particular properties are stated, thereby the justification of a value-judgment would be methodologically identical with the empirical justification of assertions. Normative words would have the same status and the same function in a sentence like the empirical justification of predications in assertions.

Yet, we can argue against the account that there is an equivalence between *descriptive* and *normative expressions,* and normative *acts* do not describe anything. Value-predicates are no names of properties, but speaker refer to criteria of application with their utterances of such words. But the interpretation of such utterances supposes the intelligibility of attitudes because the value-judgment is open to corrections.

Why must evaluative and non-evaluative attitudes be distinguished?

The difference between both attitudes consists in the semantical properties of expressions and also the claim of reasoning that we expect of its *justification.* We do not explain evaluative beliefs in the same way in which we explain the consent of assertions.

But how do we verify the acceptance of evaluative ascriptions?

We investigate these ascriptions hypothetically at our own value-attitudes. We can express our non-cognitive states, such as, emotions and wants. This is a matter of a capacity of natural speaker to ascribe evaluative attitudes exemplified on given occasions in his *own* culture. But we can only dispose about this capacity if we have learned how to modify our own self-ascriptions of attitudes. Propositional attitudes are to redescribe as *objective* because they have a semantic content. This is also valid for conative attitudes.[50] The utterance of a commitment or being committed is also to re-interpret as a *belief* and not only as a *subjective preference* or *affection*; and we do not make demands on any reasoning of such beliefs. This is the feature that explains why commit-

50 Nida-Rümelin, Ethische Essays, 16-20.

ments take effect. It is possible that beliefs are shattered, but it is one of their essential features that we have no doubts about them. Yet, beliefs and commitments have fulfillment conditions and, as such, do not stand alone. From experience we know that expectations may be disappointed, but there are no commitments without which we project them into the future of the social intercourse. There are no expectations without anticipation of beliefs, beliefs about actions and expectations, and also preferences of members of groups. This is common among sociologists. Beliefs and commitments are connected within this frame of reference that we apply when redescribing and ascribing propositional attitudes.

Now in sum we conclude that the attribution and ascription of action is caused by our talk and learning of action. In this field we take in also our practical reasoning and ethical learning, and we could perceive by our attention that the theoretical, practical, moral-psychological, and social philosophy is linked.

Many philosophers agree that *reasons* are always *incomplete*, they are *irreducibly multiple*, and *genuine moral dilemmas* are not disputed. There is no *ultimate rationality*. If we recognize conflicts between our reasons, this is not decided by the reasons themselves. Only the principle of decision (exclusionary reasons) or a vindication of my/our choice is to apply by the way of life I/we have decided to live. In the first case, this may lead to deliberations about consequences or intrinsic valuable actions or, in the second case, to a hierarchy of decisions with is limited by the membership and structure of social systems. We are gradually but not absolutely free, and this is valid also for our rational choice. However, situations may occur where we utter the well-known sentence *Give me chastity and continence, only not yet* (St. Augustine).

References

Anscombe, E., Intention. Oxford 1997.

Aristotle, Nicomachean Ethics. Ed. and trans. by Martin Ostwald. New York 1962.

Armstrong, D.M., N. Malcolm, Consciousness and Causality. Oxford 1984.

Aune, B., Reason and Action. Dordrecht 1977.

— Formal Logic and Practical Reasoning. Theory of Decision 20 1986.

— Metaphysics. The Elements. Minneapolis (1985) 2002⁵.

Austin, J.L., A Plea for Excuses. Proceedings of Aristotelian Society Vol. 57 1959. Rep. in: A.L. White (ed.) The Philosophy of Action. London 1968.

— How to do Things with Words. Oxford 1962.

Ayer, A.J., Man as a Subject for Science, August Comte Memorial Lecture 6. London 1964.

Baier, K., From the Moral Point of View. A Rational Basis of Ethics (1958). New York 1965.

Bhargava, R., Individualism in Social Science. Forms and Limits of a Methodology. Oxford 1992.

Bilgrami, A., Belief and Meaning. The Unity and Locality of Mental Content. Cambridge, Mass 1992.

Borg, E., Minimal Semantics. Oxford 2004.

Brink, D.O., Moral Realism and the Sceptical Arguments from Disagreement and Queerness. Australian Journal of Philosophy 62 1984.

Burg, T., Individualism and the Mental (1979). In: Foundation of Mind. Oxford 2007.

— Two Thought Experiments Reviewed (1982). In: Burge 2007.

— Cartesian Error and the Objectivity of Perception (1986). In: Burge 2007.

— Truth Thought Reason Essays On Frege. Oxford 2005.

— Postscript to Individualism and the Mental 2006. In: Burge 2007.

Cappelen, H., E. Lepore, Insensitive Semantics. A Defense of Semantic Minimalism and Speech Act Pluralism. Malden 2005.

Chant, S.R., A Dilemma for Non-Reductionist Accounts of Group Belief. Forthcoming.

Dancy, J., Moral Realism. Oxford 1993.

Danto, A., Analytical Philosophy of Action. Cambridge 1973.

Davidson, D., Action, Reasons, and Causes (1963). In: Actions and Events, Oxford 1980.
— The Logical Form of Action Sentences (1967). In: Davidson 1980.
— The Individuation of Events (1969). In: Davidson 1980.
— Agency (1971). In: Oxford 1980.
— How is Weakness of the Will Possible (1970). In: Davidson 1980.
— Hempel on Explaining Action (1976). In: Davidson 1980.
— Intending (1978). In: Davidson 1980.
— On Saying That (1968). In: Truth and Interpretation. Oxford 1984.
— Thought and Talk (1975). In: Truth and Interpretation. Oxford 1984.
— The Centrality of Truth. In: J. Peregrin (ed.) Truth and its Nature if any. London 1999.
— Epistemology and Truth (1988). In: Subjective, Intersubjective, Objective. Oxford 2001.
— Empirical Content (1982). In: Davidson 2001.
— Three Varieties of Knowledge (1992). In: Davidson 2001.
— The Second Person (1992). In: Davidson 2001.
— The Emergence of Thoughts (1997). In: Davidson 2001.
— Paradoxes of Irrationality (1982). In: Problems of Rationality. Oxford 2004.
— Expressing Evaluation (1984), Appendix: Objectivity and Practical Reasoning (2000). In: Davidson 2004.
— The Interpersonal Comparison of Values (1986). In: Davidson 2004.
— Problems in the Explanation of Action (1987). In: Davidson 2004.
— The Objectivity of Values (1995). In: Davidson 2004.
— Could There Be a Science of Rationality? (1995). In: Davidson 2004.
— Law and Cause (1995). In: Truth, Language, and History. Oxford 2005.
— Aristotle's Action (2001). In: Davidson 2005.
Ducasse, C. J., Nature, Mind, and Death. Illinois 1951.

Edwards, S., Externalism in the Philosophy of Mind. Brookfield 1994.
Elster, J., The Nature and Scope of Rational Choice Explanation. In: E. Lepore, MacLaughlin (eds.), Action and Events. Perspectives on the Philosophy of D. Davidson. New York 1985.
Essler, W. K., Was ist Wahrheit. In: G. Preyer et al. (eds.). Language, Mind, and Epistemology. On Donald Davidson's Philosophy. Dordrecht 1994.
— Theorie und Erfahrung. Eine Einführung in die Wissenschaftstheorie, Freiburg Br. 2000.
— Unser die Welt. Sprachphilosophische Grundlegungen der Erkenntnistheorie. Ausgewählte Artikel. Ed. by G. Preyer, Frankfurt am Main 2001.

Feinberg, J., Action and Responsibility (1965). In: A. L. White (ed.), Philosophy of Action. London 1968.

Fodor, J., Psychosemantic. Cambridge 1987.

— LOT 2 The Language of Thought Revisited. Oxford 2008.

Frankfurt, H., Freedom of the Will and the Concept of the Person. Journal of Philosophy Vol. 68 1 1971.

Geach, G., Ascriptivism. In Logic Matter. Oxford 1992.

Gilbert, M., Sociality and Responsibility. New Essays in Plural Subject Theory, Lanham 2000.

Goldman, A. I., A Theory of Human Action. Englewood Cliff 1970.

— The Individuation of Action. Journal of Philosophy LXVIII 1971.

— Folk Psychology and Mental Concepts. ProtoSociology Vol. 14 2000: Folk Psychology, Mental Concepts and the Ascription of Attitudes. On Contemporary Philosophy of Mind.

Hamsphire, S., Thought and Action. New York 1959.

Hart, H.. L. A., The Ascription of Responsibility and Rights In: Proceedings of Aristotelian Society XLIX 1949.

Honore, A. M., Causation in Law. London 1959.

Henrich, D., Ethik des Nuclearen Friedens. Frankfurt am Main 1990.

— Selbstbewußtsein. Hermeneutik und Dialektik. Bd. 1. Hrsg. R. Bubner. Tübingen 1970.

— Denken und Selbstsein. Frankfurt am Main 2008.

Hornsby, J., Actions. London 1980.

Kim, J., Events as Property Exemplifications. In: Supervenience and Mind. Selected Philosophical Essays. Cambridge GB 1993.

— Noncausal Connections. In: Kim 1993.

— Psychophysical Laws. In: Supervenience and Mind. Selected Philosophical Essays. Oxford 1993.

Krawietz, W., Risiko, Recht und normative Verantwortung. Recht und Natur. Beiträge zu Ehren von Friedrich Kaulbach. Hrsg. von V. Gerhardt, W. Krawietz. Schriften zur Rechtstheorie, Heft 153 1992.

Kulenkampff, A., F. Siebelt, Noncognitivist might tell a Moral Realist. ProtoSociology Vol. 14 2000: Folk Psychology, Mental Concepts and the Ascription of Attitudes. On Contemporary Philosophy of Mind.

Lawrence, P. R., J. W. Lorsch, Organization and Environment: Managing Differentiation and Integration. Boston 1967.

Lehrer, K., Knowledge. Oxford 1994.

Lepore, E., The Compositionality Papers. Oxford 2002.

Lepore, E., K. Ludwig, Donald Davidson. Meaning, Truth, Language, and Reality. Oxford 2005.

Loar, B., Social Content and Psychological Content. In: R.H. Grimm, D. Merrill (eds.), Contents of Thoughts. Tucson 1988.

— A new Kind of Content. In: Grimm, Merrill 1988.

Ludwig, L., The Truth about Moods. In: G. Preyer, G. Peter, M. Ulkan (eds.), Concepts of Meaning. Framing an Integrated Theory of Linguistic Behavior. Dordrecht 2003.

Luhmann, N., Das Recht der Gesellschaft. Frankfurt am Main 1993.

MacIntyre, A.C., A Mistake about Causality in Social Science. In: P. Laslett, W.G. Runciman (eds.), Philosophy, Politics and Sociology II. Oxford 1962.

Macdonald, C., Mind-Body Identity Theories. London 1989.

— Weak Externalism and Mind-body Identity. Mind Vol. 99 1990.

— Weak Externalism and Psychological Reduction. In: D. Charles, K. Lennon (eds.), Reduction, Explanation and Realism. Oxford 1992.

MacDonald, G., P. Pettit, Semantics and Social Science. London 1981.

Malpas, J. (ed.), Dialogues with Davidson. Cambridge MA. 2011.

Martin, R.M., Events, Reference and Logical Form. Washington D.C. 1978.

McDowell, J., Are Moral Requirements Hypothetical Imperatives? In: McDowell (ed.), Mind, Value, and Reality. Cambridge 1998.

McGinn, C., The Structure of Content. In: A. Woodfield (ed.), Thought and Object. Oxford 1982.

— The Subjective View. Oxford 1982.

— The Character of Mind. Oxford 1982.

— Mental Content. Oxford 1989.

McNaughton, D., Moral Vision. Oxford 1988.

Malcolm, N., Consciousness and Causality. In: D. M. Armstrong, Norman Malcolm Consciousness and Causality. Oxford 1984.

Meggle, G., M. Ulkan, Informatives and/Or Directives? A New Start in Speech Act Classification. In: G. Preyer, G. Peter and M. Ulkan (eds.), Concepts of Meaning. Framing an Integrated Theory of Linguistic Behavior. Dordrecht 2003.

Melden, A.I., Free Action. London 1960.

— Willing (1960). In: A.R. White (ed.), Philosophy of Action. Oxford 1968.

Mele, A.R., Springs of Action. Understanding intentional Behavior. Oxford 1992.

— Self-Deception Unmasked. Princeton 2001.

— Effective Intention. The Power of Conscious Will. Oxford 2009.

— Miguens, S., Rationality, Belief, Desire: a Research Program. In: Miguens, C. E. E. Mauro (eds.), Perspectives on Rationality. Porto 2006.
— Concepts of Belief, Triangulation and Joint Attention. In: Miguens, Mauro (eds.) 2006.

Neale, S., Facing Facts. Oxford 2001.
Nida-Rümelin, J., Kritik des Konsequentialismus. München 1995.
— The Plurality of Good Reasons and the Theory of Practical Rationality. In: Preyer, Peter (eds.), The Contextualization of Rationality. Problems, Concepts and Theories of Rationality. Perspectives in Analytical Philosophy. New Series. Edited by G. Meggle and J. Nida-Rümelin. Paderborn 2000.
— Strukturelle Rationalität. Ein philosophisches Essay über praktische Vernunft. Stuttgart 2001.
— Ethische Essays. Frankfurt am Main 2002.
— Über menschliche Freiheit. Stuttgart 2005.
Nida-Rümelin, M., Der Blick von innen. Zur transtemporalen Identität bewusstseinsfähiger Wesen. Frankfurt am Main 2006.

O'Shaughnessy, B., Trying (As the Mental Pineal Gland), 52, 65. In: Mele (ed.), Philosophy of Action, Oxford 1997.

Peters, R. S., The Concept of Motivation, London 1958.
Pettit, P., A Theory of Freedom. From the Psychology to the Politics of Agency, Cambridge 2001.
Pietroski, P., Semantics and Metaphysics of Events. In: K. Ludwig (ed.), Davidson. Cambridge 2003.
Platts, M., Ways of Meaning. An Introduction to a Philosophy of Language. London 1979.
— Moral Reality and the End of Desire. In: Platts (eds.), Truth and Reality. Essay on the Philosophy of Language. London 1980.
Pollock, J. L., Knowledge and Justification. Princeton 1974.
Preyer, G., Review: Ein Meister aus dem Norden. R. Tuomela, Philosophy of Social Practices. The Collective Acceptance View. Cambridge 2002. In: Philosophische Rundschau 4 2003.
— Review: R. Tuomela, Cooperations. Philosophical Series 82. Dordrecht 2000. In: Philosophischer Literaturanzeiger 1 2004.
— Verstehen, Referenz, Wahrheit: Über Hilary Putnams Philosophie. In: Interpretation, Sprache und das Soziale (1997). Philosophische Aufsätze. Frankfurt am Main 2005.
— Interpretation, Sprache und das Soziale. Philosophische Artikel (Interpretation, Language, and the Social. Philosophical Articles). Frankfurt am Main 2005.

— Donald Davidson's Philosophy. From Radical Interpretation to Radical Contextualism. Frankfurt am Main 2011[2].

— Review: R. Rosenthal, Consciousness and Mind, Oxford 2005. Philosophischer Literaturanzeiger 3/4 2006.

— What a Theory of Action is possible?, Rechtstheorie 4 2006.

— Review: T. Burg, Foundation of Mind, Oxford 2007. Philosophischer Literaturanzeiger 4 2007.

— Soziologische Theorie der Gegenwartsgesellschaft (3 vols.), Mitgliedschafttheoretische Untersuchungen I, Lebenswelt, System, Gesellschaft II, Mitgliedschaft und Evolution III. Wiesbaden 2006, 2006, 2008.

— Review: T. Burge, Truth Thought Reason Essays On Frege, Oxford 2005. Philosophischer Literaturanzeiger 1 2009.

— Evaluative Attitudes. In: J. Malpas (ed.), Dialogues with Davidson: Dialogues with Davidson: Acting, Interpreting, Understanding. Cambridge MA. 2011.

Preyer, G., F. Siebelt, Reality and Humean Supervenience: Some Reflections on David Lewis' Philosophy. In: Reality and Humean Supervenience. Edited and Introduced by G. Preyer and F. Siebelt. Lanham 2001.

Preyer, G., G. Peter (eds.), Contextualism in Philosophy. Knowledge, Meaning, and Truth. Oxford 2005.

— Context-Sensitivity and Semantic Minimalism Essays on Semantics and Pragmatics. Oxford 2007.

Prichard, H. A., Action, Willing, Desiring. In: Moral Obligations. Oxford 1949.

ProtoSociology An International Journal of Interdisciplinary Research Vol. 21 2005: Compositionality, Concepts and Representations. New Problems in Cognitive Science I. ProtoSociology Vol. 22 2006: Compositionality, Concepts and Representations. New Problems in Cognitive Science II.

Putnam, H., The Meaning of Meaning (1975). In: Language, Mind and Knowledge: Minnesota Studies in the Philosophy of Science, Vol. 7. Ed. K. Gunderson. Minnesota 1975.

Quine, W. v. O., Word and Object. Cambridge Mass. 1964.

Raz, J., Practical Reason and Norms. London 1978.

— Introduction. In: Raz (ed.), Practical Reasoning. Oxford 1978.

Recanati, F., Literal Meaning. Cambridge 2004.

Rescher, N., Aspects of Action. In: Rescher (ed.), The Logic of Decision and Action. Pittburg 1967.

— Rationalität. Würzburg 1993.

Rogler, E., G. Preyer, Anomalous Monism and Mental Causality. On the

Debate of Donald Davidson's Philosophy of the Mental, Frankfurt am Main 2004, https://ssl.humanities-online.de/en/openaccess.php
— Anomaler Monismus und mentale Kausalität: Ein Beitrag zur Debatte über D. Davidsons Philosophie des Mentalen. In: Materialismus, anomaler Monismus und mentale Kausalität. Zur gegenwärtigen Philosophie des Mentalen bei D. Davidson und D. Lewis. Frankfurt am Main 2001.
Röska-Hardy, L., Internalism, Externalism, and Davidson's Conception of the Mental. In: G. Preyer et al. (eds.) Language, Mind and Epistemology. On D. Davidson's Philosophy. Dordrecht 1994.
— Die Rolle von Sprache und Selbstwissen. In: A. Newen, G. Vosgeran (Hrsg.), Den eigenen Geist kennen. Paderborn 2005.
Rosenthal, R., Consciousness and Mind. Oxford 2005.
Ryle, G., Concept of Mind. New York 1949.

Schantz, R., Wahrheit, Referenz und Realismus. Eine Studie zur Sprachphilosophie und Metaphysik. Berlin 1996.
Schnädelbach, H., Analytische und Postanalytische Philosophie. Vorträge und Abhandlungen 4. Frankfurt am Main 2004.
Searle, J. R., Rationality in Action, Cambridge 2001.
Sellars, V. Thought and Action. In: K. Lehrer (ed.), Freedom and Determinism. New York 1966.
— Science and Metaphysics. London 1968.
— Action and Events. Nous 7 1973.
Shackle, G. I. S., Imagination, Formalism, and Choice. In: M. J. Rizzo (ed.), Time, Uncertainty, and Disequilibrium: Explorations in Austrian Theme. Lexington Mass. 1979.
Stegmüller, W., Probleme und Resultate der Wissenschaftstheorie und Analytischen Philosophie, Bd. 1. Erklärung, Begründung, Kausalität. Berlin 1983: 487-92.
Stevenson, C. L., Ethic and Language. New York 1944.
Stoutland, F., The Logical Connection Argument. American Philosophical Quarterly 7 1970.
Strawson, P. F., Freedom and Resentment. In: Proceedings of the British Academy 1962.
Shwayder, D. S., The Stratification of Behaviour. A System of Definitions Propounded and Defended. New York 1965.

Taylor, C., Explanation of Behavior. London 1964.
— Human Agency and Language. Cambridge 1985.
Thalberg, I., Do we cause our own Actions? Analysis 27 1967.
Thompson, J. J., G. Harman, Moral Realism and Moral Objectivity. Cambridge Mass. 1996.
Toulmin, S. E., Human Understanding. Princton 1972.

Tugendhat, E., Selbstbewußtsein und Selbstbestimmung. Sprachanalytische Interpretationen. Frankfurt am Main 1979.

Tuomela, R., Human Action and Its Explanation. Dordrecht 1977.

— Cooperations. Philosophical Series 82. Dordrecht 2000.

— Philosophy of Social Practices. The Collective Acceptance View. Cambridge 2002.

— The Philosophy of Sociality. The Shared Point of View, Oxford 2007.

— On Individualism and Collectivism in Social Science. Forthcoming.

Wilson, G., The Intentionality of Human Action. Stanford 1989.

Wittgenstein, L., Philosophical Investigations. Oxford 1953.

Wright, G. H. von, Practical Inference. Philosophical Review 72 1963.

— On so-called Practical Inference (1959). In: Raz (ed.), Practical Reasoning. Oxford 1978.

— Normen, Werte und Handlungen. Frankfurt am Main 1994.

— Das Verstehen von Handlungen—Disputation mit Georg Meggle. In: Wright 1994.

Weaver, B. W., Science and Complexity, American Scientist 36 1948.

Wunderlich, W., Studien zur Sprechakttheorie. Frankfurt am Main 1976.

Name Index

Subject Index

www.ingramcontent.com/pod-product-compliance
Lightning Source LLC
Chambersburg PA
CBHW031445280326
41927CB00037B/358